Some early endorsements

Thanks for sending the copy of your book… There's a whole life's work poured in. I must say that your chapter on punishment may be the most succinct chapter I've read on the subject. Thanks for your clarity there. Thanks for letting me know of your endeavor. May your book reach many, and change their lives.

–In solidarity, Patty Wipfler

I get the feeling that it might become your best book ever! Because it's such a tremendously fundamental topic! I've worked with children long enough to recognize what you're talking about: I've also felt the same as you describe when going for a walk with a three-year old (but even with smaller children). What I find particularly important is that – because of a yet undeveloped language – children "force" us to utilize other means of communication, among others intonation and joy! Lightness might be another connection. For, although children can be very serious about their play, there is also very much lightness involved. That's an area I like to explore more in depth, seeing how playfulness and lightness can be linked to – and perhaps ultimately lead to – wisdom.

–Claudio Manfredi

OK, so I am crying by the dedication. Solely because it is being said. Almost like validation for everything. I love your voice, because I know you... I liked hearing about you and your mother, the closeness, I could feel it. It was interesting to me, what you said about nature vs. nurture, how that question would not apply to other species. Never thought of that, but you are right. We are part of nature. We are natural. In turn we are also a part of natural selection. Do we think it would not apply to us?

I found joy in the end of the story, the children bring us hope, joy, wonder, connection, love, trust, etc. We learn from them and them from us, in a circle that bonds and strengthens. If we can live alongside the child, we are privileged to be part of this joyous and wondrous path of life. What a blessing! Thanks for sharing.

–Jennifer Mésquita

Successful Native Rearing Wisdom

I knew a man who raised excellent hunting dogs. When asked why he had such good dogs, he simply answered that he played with them and talked to them. Child raising is very similar to how he raised such impressive dogs.

Native Peoples placed the highest regard, duty of their lives on Child Care. They followed Nature's teachings explicitly for their lifestyle, Religious, Spiritual, Social and Political. What Nature showed them, revealed to them – they dutifully followed.

The primary goal of 'The Moving Ones' – Wamaskaskan – Animal World (Sioux) was the right upbringing, protection, preparation and survival of their young. For the Animal World such duty was rather simple; it was engrained by the Creator. Therefore Two-legged needed to have this Duty religiously/Spiritually followed; as simple and obviously rewarding as could be.

–Response of EagleMan, Ed McGaa, Lakota, to this book

The Joy of Caring for Children in The Circle Way
(It Takes a Child to Raise a Village)

Also by Manitonquat (Medicine Story)

Non-Fiction
Return to Creation
Ending Violent Crime
The Circle Way
Changing the World
The Original Instructions
Have You Lost Your Tribe?

Fiction
Children of the Morning Light
Wampanoag Morning
The Granddaughter of the Moon

Poetry
Grandfather Speaks
Birch Cottage
Come Home

The Joy of Caring for Children in The Circle Way

(It Takes a Child to Raise a Village)

by Manitonquat (Medicine Story)

STORY STONE PUBLISHING

The Joy of Caring for Children in The Circle Way
by Manitonquat (Medicine Story)

Copyright © 2015 Manitonquat (Medicine Story)
All rights reserved.
ISBN-13: 978-1506179780
ISBN-10: 1506179789
BISAC: Family & Relationships / Parenting / General

Story Stone Publishing
167 Merriam Hill Road, Greenville, NH 03048
First printing.

Design: Beechleaf Design

www.circleway.org

Dedication

I would like to dedicate this book to my wife Ellika, my partner, chief supporter, colleague and co-teacher through all the years of developing this work,

and to Emmy Rainwalker – just observing her interactions with children in our care has been the most continuous and significant teaching of this work for me,

to our sons Tokeem and Tashin, who are thoughtful and playful allies to their own and all children, and to their wives Tanja and Frieda, paradigms of caring motherhood to our grandchildren,

to Tim Jackins, Patty Wipfler, and Chuck Esser, who have directly inspired and informed our work in community and camps, and who continue to teach and model by their lives, their thinking, their respect for young people, and their playfulness,

to Jenny Sazama who in her lifelong advocacy for young people has taught me so much,

to our friend Elena Balsamo who is carrying the inspiration of Maria Montessori to a new level in our society today and who urged me to write this book,

to our old friends Wavy Gravy and Patch Adams who embody in their activities the humor and the play and the culture-shattering genius of the clown that all children love and that inspires the child in all of us,

and

to all mothers and fathers everywhere who continually work to make a better childhood and a better world for all children.

In Grateful Memory of
Maria Montessori
(1870-1952) Physician and Educator

Quotes from this pioneer in the teaching of children:

> "The study of love and its utilization will lead us to the source from which it springs, the Child."

> "Each child needs among other things: care, protection, security, warmth, skin contact, touching, caressing, and tenderness."

> "When dealing with a child there is greater need for observing than probing."

> "Free choice is one of the highest of mental processes."

> "Never help a child with a task at which he feels he can succeed."

> "Character formation cannot be taught. It comes from experience and not from explanation."

In Grateful Memory of
Alice Miller
(1923-2010) Psychologist, Philosopher, Sociologist

Quotes from a pioneer in the revelation of the abuse of children, that it is "not limited to physical and sexual assault but includes any attack, such as derision, shaming, humiliation, neglect, deception and manipulation."

> "If I succeed in my books in reaching a few people who were fortunate enough to have had an enlightened witness in their childhood, even if only for a very short time, they will become conscious witnesses and advocates of children."

> "As long as feelings are not felt, the self-damaging blockages remain."

> "The goal of therapy is to allow the once silenced child in us to speak and feel."

> "What has he learned from this punishment other than to dissemble and, later, likewise to resort to violence and to avenge himself on his children?"

> "For their development children need the respect and protection of adults who take them seriously, love them, and honestly help them become oriented in the world."

Contents

Author's Preface 15
Introduction 19
Prologue: How Death Came in the World 33

Part One 37
Chapter One: About Our Nature 39
Chapter Two: About You, The Adult 58
Chapter Three: Relating to Children in General 73

Part Two 93
Chapter Four: Play Time 95
Chapter Five: Special Time 112
Chapter Six: The Art of Listening 123

Part Three 135
Chapter Seven: Punishment 137
Chapter Eight: Control 139
Chapter Nine: Setting Limits 153

Part Four 167
Chapter Ten: The Circle Way 169
Chapter Eleven: Parents Liberation 185
Chapter Twelve: The Village 200

Epilogue: The Story of Muckachuck 221

Appendix 227
Bibliography 267
Resources 271

> *"Let us put our minds together and see what life we can make for our children."*
>
> —attributed to Sitting Bull (1832-1890)

> *"If a child is to keep alive his inborn sense of wonder, he needs the companionship of at least one adult who can share it, rediscovering with him the joy, excitement, and mystery of the world we live in."*
>
> —Rachel Carson (1907-1964)

Author's Preface

This book is rooted in the soil of the traditional ways of caring for children of our First Nations communities in North America, as I have in my travels observed them among parents in various of those communities that have managed to retain these ways more or less uncontaminated by the invading European attitudes that were so disrespectful of children. That circle way of community caring for children has been little documented in print, and it was a primary interest for me as I travelled in my youth, listening to elders and family members of all ages across the US and Canada.

Out of that soil my wife Ellika and I have for many years cultivated in our family workshops and camps the growth of cooperative caring for children, of parents helping each other to give the best of themselves to their children and each other using the approach and techniques of Re-Evaluation Counseling in a blend we call The Circle Way. A further goal to enlarge the scope of that caring will be found in the final two chapters of the book, namely of Parents Liberation and the creation of new communities that return to our indigenous values of cooperation, sharing, caring for each person from child to elder, together caring for all beings, all life, and for our beloved Mother Earth.

Of the dozen books I have committed to print this latest is by far the most important to me, one that condenses the essence of what I have sought and learned in my 85 years on this Earth. The legacy I most urgently want to pass on to the world. I hope you may find it important to you. My other books have been directed at the network that has grown around my work, people who are interested perhaps in Native American traditional wisdom but also in the quality as well as the very survival of life on this planet.

Children today are entering a society that is hostile to them, that ignores their thinking and feelings as valuable human beings, values them only for the profit of industries, turns them into competitors who are measured on Procrustean beds of a common standard, drugs them when they do not conform, and offers little help to parents struggling to find ways to provide a home, food, and health and have time to spend getting close, playing with and guiding their children as they grow.

More than ever before in history human beings are becoming urgently concerned about a vast need for social change, the need to end war and violence, the need to save life from ecological disaster, the need to extend political freedom and protection, adequate housing, provenance, and medical care to all people. And a wish to see realized the foundation of all religions and social thought, universal compassion and caring.

This movement that now raises its head and looks about to join its unknown members, sometimes called The Great Change, or The Great Turning, has been my dream and my guide in growing awareness through the past 60 years. This book is the result of what I have learned and worked at, and its culmination is here, in how we will raise the future generations of human beings to their full potentiality. I want here to clarify an essential tool for this movement, a movement that will, if heeded, transform the world and fulfill the human dream of love and joy through the joy and love of our children, ever our guides as we guide them.

You and I have the power to affect the future of humankind with every interaction we have with a child. With adults as well, but our power and influence is greatest with children. We have the most power as parents, and then as allies to parents, as grandparents, teachers, counselors, and as friends to all children. Only a few minutes being with any child, listening to them, playing with them, showing them their value and importance to you and to everyone, giving them a larger picture of life and of themselves to contradict the negative messages of others, will bring more connection into their lives. That will have a powerful effect on those children, give them an experience of understanding and compassion to strengthen and illuminate their journeys through life.

My elders taught us to consider our actions as affecting the unborn generations that we will never know. This book contains the rudiments of what I have learned to best do that.

Beyond that, I would like all of us to make children our priority, put them at the center of our thoughts, feelings and actions, return childhood to children, enhance the joys of play and connection, and of nature, the wonder and delight of learning and the marvels in every moment of awareness. I say this not just for them, but also when we do that they enrich our own lives, our learning, and our joy beyond measure.

Introduction

A young woman friend of ours had made excellent grades in high school and intended to go to college to become an engineer. But after graduation she decided to take a break from academics for a while and took a job that involved caring for and working with children. Later she entered the university, but the studies bored her and the prospect of a future working as an engineer depressed her. Remembering the joy her work with the children had given her, she quit, took up studying caring for children, and later went to work in that field, where she is happily employed today. All her friends told her she was crazy to give up such a respectable, high quality career with wonderful opportunities for advancement only to work with children, which is ill paid and carries little prestige.

You can see by this story how twisted the values of our culture have become. The work with the children still brings joy to our friend, as well as to all the children and their families, and has a positive effect on society and on all those who will be affected by the love and happiness of those children as they grow and raise children of their own.

There is a revolution under way in caring for children, similar to those that have gained so much in human rights, as in the case of sexism, racism, classism, colonialism, and in all other assaults on equality and human dignity. All the money in the world cannot equal the good of such love and joy added to the life of even a single child.

This revolution is in part merely a return, to recreate the more human relationships that were the fabric of life for most primitive communities and of indigenous peoples as I have experienced them, that even today hold and honor the integrity and sacredness of those relationships.

This book begins an examination and discussion of these relationships such as I have learned from elders of my own people and from developing them in the family camps and workshops we work with today.

Children are People

But first a caveat. This book was written by a fellow who, although he has had a long career as a teacher and educator, a community builder and author, a father and grandfather, has never fully 'grown up', and he is now a garrulous old codger of eighty-five who, like many of that ilk, will wander down memory lane without compunction and repeat himself often. (Repetition is necessary for teaching, but of course his generally excellent memory is not exactly infallible.)

I have consciously re-read and re-written however, and come to the decision that this rambling on is the price you must pay for all this good information. (As Bernard Shaw said of one of his letters to Mrs. Pat Campbell, if I had more time I would have written it shorter.)

Okay, here we go: another book by another self-proclaimed expert in the raising of children. But you ought to watch out: experts often have a bias. And I have a bias, of course. And I will try to tell you my bias here so you can decide how you want to take what I have to say.

Because, you understand, I believe there are really only two experts in this child caring enterprise. One of them is the parent and the other is the child. I am committed whole-heartedly to be on the side of the child, and I definitely am on the side of every parent. If you are not a parent but are reading this as a caregiver, a teacher or counselor, I want to encourage you also to be an ally to all children and all parents, as I seek to be.

So I have a bias. It is toward what some people call "natural" child care, the kind that evolved in the hundred thousand or so years of the socialization of our species, not in every culture, but at least in the one that I am most familiar with, the traditional culture of my own ancestors in North America. I am convinced of this style because of my personal experience in several traditional communities of First Nation peoples in America, and the first hand reports of indigenous families I have met from other parts of the world, and also from written reports such as those of Sonbofu Somé, Jean Liedloff, Bruce Chatwin, Laurens Van Der Post, and many others.

My bias is in direct opposition to those I notice operating in about every culture in the world today, which, in my opinion, is the main reason for the mess the world is in. One bias I am opposed to is the one that thinks that babies, cute as the may be, are ignorant and will not learn unless we teach them, and that they are tiresome extra burdens that soon turn into thoughtless little monsters making as much mess and noise and work for us as they can, and who evolve eventually into sullen, resentful and completely incomprehensible teenagers, after which they hopefully leave home and become other people's problems.

There are other biases I do not share. The one that says young people today are out of control, worse than they ever were in our day, so give up, they just have to learn the hard way. Or the one that says kids have to be punished when they misbehave – that's the only way to keep them in line, as in "my parents were tough – you have to lay down the law and enforce it or kids will run all over you."

All these ideas stem from an old one that human nature is deeply flawed and unless we control it from the beginning with threats of punishment and retribution it will run amok with greed and selfishness and cruelty.

My bias is the opposite: that human nature is benign, and when a child's needs are met, needs for safety and security, for nourishment, for belonging and acceptance, for appreciation and love, children will love because that is their nature. It is in their nature to want to be like their caregivers, and they will be cooperative and caring of others because we are. That is also their nature, and they will want to learn and create things that give them a sense of pride and accomplishment.

That's what I believe, and my belief is reinforced by much research that confirms the effectiveness of these new approaches and by the multitude of experts writing of new approaches to child rearing. Also by my experience as a father and a teacher/educator of many, many children from birth through to adulthood, as well as my experience as a personal counselor for over forty years, including hearing the stories of abuse and neglect in childhood from all the prisoners I have counseled for three decades.

These new approaches are already making a great difference for children in many parts of the world, but the stresses and the isolation created by modern society have all but destroyed the support that parents once had from extended families and communities that are no longer there for them. This subject – the support for parents and other child-care givers –is one basic motivation for my writing this book.

I take the opportunity to add another voice to the many good books available today on caring for children (I will add a bibliography of some of my favorites) but I am adding some insights from the family work of the international organization of Re-evaluation Counseling for over 50 years. Developed by my friends Tim Jackins, Patty Wipfler, and Chuck Esser, inspiring what Ellika and I present in our camps every year, their work deserves to be much better known to the general public.

The ways referred to in this book are not theoretical, but based on the experience of many care-givers as well as my own experience in teaching and caring for children, with raising my own children in a community dedicated to these ways, seeing how these ways work with children in the family camps my wife and I have conducted every summer for fifteen years, and reading reports from all over the world of successes people are having in using these ways.

If you don't agree with this approach, if you do it differently, that will not make you a bad child-carer and will not in itself make for unhappy children. If you love the children and follow your heart as my elders taught, all will be well. Even so I think you may find some ideas here helpful and encouraging.

It is finally being realized in contemporary thinking that children are people and that treating them with complete respect physically, mentally, emotionally is best for all society, and even better to treat them with affection, compassion, and understanding, benefiting both adults and children. Hopefully this revolution will include the liberation of parents, who do the most important work in this world and receive little or no acknowledgement or support for it.

The ideas I want to play around with here in this book will possibly seem obvious and commonsensical to some and disturbingly radical to others. I hope the former understand they still have a lot to learn. I still have a lot to learn, even though I know and write about this subject, the practice is not obvious or easy, but I get better the more I push myself to play with it. For the latter group – well, all I can say is that the world offered to children today gets low marks in humanity across the board. Violence, drugs, crime, greed, materialism, selfishness, isolation, loneliness, apathy do not comprise a healthy environment for children, and that doesn't even include war, poverty, hunger, pollution, environmental degradation, oppression, sexual abuse, and plain meanness... No need to go on. We all want a better world for our children to grow in – and we can give it to them.

The ideas and practices described in this book are working. Right now, as I write this and as you read it, there are groups of people around the world, many I know personally, some in which I am actively participating, that are working together to create the kind of villages it takes to raise a child in the very best way our hearts and minds can devise.

For thirty-five years I have been making circles with prisoners in the United States, counseling and listening to men and women who have committed a wide range of crimes, and I can tell you that not one of those prisoners had a decent childhood. They were all, essentially abused or abandoned, sometimes both. They were all born, as all human children are everywhere in the world, wanting to be cared about lovingly and thoughtfully. They wanted to explore and learn and connect to others, wanted to play and have fun and laugh. They needed to be safe, nurtured, understood and appreciated for the marvelous little beings they were, every one. They needed to know they belong here.

It was not their fault that they became criminals. We say the crimes were their choices, and as a society we tend to blame them – but they did not choose those paths. They were abandoned to those paths by us, by a society that failed them, failed to nurture and guide them as they needed and deserved. As it had also failed to care for and guide their parents and their families. Like Alice Miller, I believe that the beginning of crime, violence, and all human evil, lies in the way that we treat our children, and that when society as a whole learns how to treat children with complete respect, compassion and understanding it will end those evils.

Since the very beginnings of civilization adults have blamed their children for their reaction to their mistreatment, as teachers blamed pupils for being poor students. And even in our enlightened era adults on the whole act as though children were something inferior, less than fully human, endowed with opposition, deliberate mischief, a desire to frustrate and impede the dictates of adults, usually attributing that to a flaw in human nature that must be corrected, excised and taught to conform to the lawful and reasonable rules of the adult. Adults fail to see themselves in their children, to remember how it was for them when they were at that age, how the world seemed, how adults treated them. They expect their children to understand the world as they see and report it, and they make no attempt to see and understand how the child sees that world and their commands.

There are things that happened to every one of us in our childhoods that we would not wish on other children today. Places where we were hurt and no one could understand. Places where we could not even cry out for help, where we were not even allowed to cry or show our hurt. And suddenly we were, at that moment, on the outside, without power, with no allies or supporters, so we took our hurt inside ourselves. Deciding there was no help, we knew we had to figure out our own survival, and sometimes our confusions led us into error.

I think everyone has at some time done something hurtful, or immoral, or even illegal, has mistreated someone and regretted it – or maybe not regretted it. Not because we were bad, or have a mean or evil streak, but because we were somewhere, as children, hurt and confused. At some point we were not given complete respect, not listened to and understood and appreciated and gently guided. We acted out of our hurt, our indignation, our confusion.

No matter how supported we were as children, there were some things that happened that we would not wish on our own children, that we would not wish on any child. Think of your own childhood. You may have blocked out the memories just to get on with your life, but were there not times when you had no help or support, times that scared you or enraged you with injustice and unfairness? Were there not things that happened that you would not want to happen in that way to your own child, or any child?

Our parents struggled with the job of parenting. Given no support from their own families and communities, with a long legacy of misunderstanding and faulty information about raising wonderful human children, they did the best they could.

Human beings need human beings.

Human beings need other human beings, connection and closeness.

A human baby growing up without human contact does not become human – witness the instances of children raised by animals. The process of learning to be fully human requires a close bonding with a single parent at first, extending then to others in the family and further to a community, a clan, a tribe, that may help and care for and guide the little one through the two decades it takes to become a fully developed adult.

That group, that circle of people, should provide safety of course, and nourishment, but also physical touch, warmth and closeness. It should provide stimulation and challenge, the freedom to explore and discover. It should provide understanding and a reflection of who they are, their natural goodness and value to the family, the tribe, the world, and to life. It should nurture confidence and self-esteem, and provide a needed sense of belonging.

In ages past everyone was born into such a circle, not only such an extended family, but also often into a clan and into a community – a tribe. It was when our humanoid ancestors came together for the first time to protect and provide for each other that they learned to cooperate, and in cooperating to communicate, and in communicating to create language, and through language developed the modern brain and became human – homo sapiens sapiens.

Most significantly those early human beings also took care of the children together. Not just as a family, but as a community. Other animals take only a year to mature and become autonomous, independent of parental care. But the complex brains of human babies take more than two decades to completely mature. The years it took for people to care for each child to adulthood affected their attitudes towards the helpless babies, the reaching infants, the young learners, and that attitude affected all relationships, including caring for those who could not care for themselves, and bestowing affection and honor upon the elders.

In our society today people are isolated, have no sense of belonging – though they long for it and strive for belonging to a nation, a flag, a club, a school or a football team, they feel little acceptance or involvement there. They have no loving, caring support system and struggle on their own. Even many tribes struggling to hold on to tradition have lost the essential human element of a circle of equals helping and caring for each other and the children together as one family, a community.

The elders from many First Nations of North America who gave me the information about the need for people to stay close to each other and help one another, to grow and live in a circle of respect and love, are all gone now, and I am an old man whose voice will not be heard for very much longer in this world. For the elders who entrusted me with this task, for the world, for the future, for all the parents and for all the children everywhere I must write this book, the most important summation of the work the elders set me to half a century ago.

The main hope I have is for our children and their children and the generations to come (we are taught by our elders to think of the consequences for seven generations beyond ours), and that what we do is for them, not for us, not for our parents, not for our therapists or authorities, not for the rules or standards of our communities, our religions, our nations, our cultures or our theories, but for our children, as the unique, special, wonderful little persons they are and will be.

I have thought about writing this book for many years. Originally it was to be called *Joyous Childraising*. Then I read Ashley Montague's thought that the word "raising" indicates that we feel that children are lower than we are and need to be raised to our level so I decided that caring was a better word. Then I thought that readers might react: "Joyous? Is he kidding? What kind of sentimental nonsense is that?" Caring for children is demanding, exhausting, flat out full time work! From pregnancy through likely the next couple of decades our search for the good life for ourselves is put on hold, put aside to attend to the needs of another being until he or she leaves the shelter of the nest we made and takes full control of his or her destiny.

I myself find a joy present throughout the cosmos. My elders spoke of the spirit singing through Creation, and creativeness continuously at play in the universe, in every story – the Song of Creation. I like that idea. All children are intent upon play – it's their job. And as a child I remember feeling very much at home in a universe whose essence was play. We find joy in the presence of children – in their innocence, in their playfulness, in their sense of justice and fairness and simple insights into the world as they find it.

This is not a new idea, unique to this book. There are many good books appearing in recent times that focus on the development of a deep and rewarding relationship between children and adults in which both are respected and honored, in which each is learning and growing through the relationship. Books that are based on the primacy of connection and caring, on attention, awareness, and compassion.

But why this book?

What have I to add to the growing literature that is not already offered there? What I want to develop here that is not so much represented in other books is something that is at the center of my world view, that was the defining gift of my life, that informs all my thinking and writing and speaking, that I seek to develop in all my work in this world, in counseling and in teaching.

In the subject of how to create community support for parents, I bring to your attention the values of my elders in the First Nations of North America. This I derived from listening to them for so many years speaking about the values of their old traditional community ways and also to many parents and grandparents who spoke of the traditional families in which they had been themselves raised. In the closely interwoven tribal circles of the past all the adults felt connected to all the children. Every baby that was born was a source of celebration and pride to all, and was assured of that sense of belonging and being cared about all their lives as children, adults, and beloved elders.

In these circumstances the mothers and fathers, who were not alone and isolated in the care of the children as parents are today, had a much easier time of it. The clans also instructed the children, and clan mothers, clan uncles or aunties were on hand to guide and help the children to be honored and loved members of the community. The familiar axiom "it takes a village to raise a child" is understandable in this context.

We are a long way from those values in our society today. Extended families living in proximity and supporting each other are a rarity, there is less than a fifty percent chance that a nuclear family will remain intact for the raising of their children to adulthood, and there is little sense of community anywhere. How then could we return to the human values in which parents are integrated and supported by a caring community?

This is the question we are undertaking to address in our camps and family workshops, using such tools as "supportive listening," "play time," "special time," and community problem solving, celebration and ceremony and others you will learn about in this book. The overall term by which we refer to all of this is The Circle Way. Using

The Circle Way in our camps and workshops we are bringing people together, contradicting the isolation and competitiveness of society to experience deep connection and the conscious creation of a truly human community in which all are supported and cared for and valued and in which the joy of working and playing and creating together is embraced by a sense of belonging.

This is the goal we will broach in the final chapter, how here and now to begin to get parents together to support each other, to create that "village" for raising our children together, to begin to live in The Circle Way.

The gift to me from my elders of the First Nations of North America, the inheritors of the old traditions of this continent, the wisdom that I found in their teaching as well in the practice of many of our people who still cling to the old ways in remote parts of the Americas, I have also found among many indigenous people honoring the way of the circle in Africa, Asia, Australia and Pacifica. Societies that live simply, grounded in love and connection with each other, with the Earth and compassion and joy in all of life, societies that keep the children at their center and ever present.

The Circle Way

We call our outreach The Circle Way from the instruction of our elders that human beings are meant to live in circles in which every person is a sacred being equally important and precious to the whole community. The Circle Way is a very practical adaptation of the principles by which all people became human during the hundred thousand or so years of living together in egalitarian circles that learned to protect, support and cooperate with each other and out of which we developed our language, our thought, and our human nature.

The Circle Way follows the way of nature. In this way we understand that the questions of nature versus nurture which have occupied us are not useful because nurture is natural and nature is nurturing. They are not questions we would apply to any other species. Only in some human cultures, such as the dominant ones we live in today, does the nurturing of children become unnatural to any mother.

The universe wants us to succeed. Natural selection wants us to produce the strongest and healthiest offspring. Strong and healthy means more than physical, it includes mental, emotional and spiritual health. Aware, curious, clear-thinking as well as emotionally balanced, happy, and creative individuals are stronger and healthier. Human beings became stronger and enhanced all those qualities as they became human by cooperating, working, learning, playing, thinking together and developing empathy – compassion.

All of those qualities are present already from birth in the human infant, and it is those qualities that we seek to enhance in each child, to be true to its nature and for its own health and happiness, as well as the continued survival and evolution of humankind.

We have learned a lot about how to nurture those qualities, and most of the books in recent times reflect that. What is less understood and hardly considered is the older wisdom contained in that axiom that it takes a village to raise a child.

That kind of village, that sense of a close-knit community, in which all members are considered parents or responsible relatives of every child, is not readily available and not even considered possible by most people. My last book, *Have You Lost Your Tribe?*, describes many communities around the world that are exploring such circles today and offers suggestions for people seeking to build their own community or ecovillage in that way. My wish in this book is to go deeper into the subject of why and how such child-centered communities are better for the children, better for the parents, better for all members, and better for the creation of a new and more human society. And I will have suggestions for how you can begin right from where you are to move in that direction. The unthinking opponents of Hillary Rodham-Clinton tried to ridicule her for proposing this notion of indigenous societies, "It takes a village to raise a child", but the thought entered the national consciousness, and most people are now at least aware of it. Still, people think, "Well, I don't have a village like that, so that's impossible anymore."

It may not be as difficult as you believe. That village, that community, is a proposition I wish to explore with you in this book, and perhaps provide you with enough encouragement and desire to empower yourself to take heart and either create or find such a community for yourself and your children. There are models. Many thousands of people and communities are engaged in this very development, which I feel is essential to the survival and evolution of human life on this planet.

For the past thirty years my wife, Ellika Lindén, and I have been making workshops and camps, including family camps, in Europe every summer, creating support for parents, children of all ages, and their allies. Ellika is a writer and director of children's theater and a co-counselor. The impetus and encouragement to write this book was provided by Elena Balsamo, an Italian pediatrician and author of books about children, who has a vision of a village dedicated to children, of families living in a circle and caring for all the children together, as in our old tribal way. After reading some of my writing about children she asked Ellika and me to lead a camp for parents and followers of her dream. I will include her vision in the appendix to this book. It was a wonderful week that we shared with their children, and it gave rise to Elena's publisher asking for a book about our work.
This is that book.

To begin I would like to share a favorite story from my people with my own coloring.

Prologue
How Death Came in the World

Maushop, Creator's helper who built the world on the back of a turtle swimming in the ocean, and who had made all the life there, the plants, the animals and the human beings, was resting by his fire late at night as the moon started to rise through the woods. Suddenly the frogs stopped singing, and he looked up to see what was the matter. There was his twin brother Matahdou, who had helped in building the world and peopling it with life but who had been banished to another world by the powers of the six directions after a terrible battle between the twins had threatened to destroy Creation. Matahdou didn't seem all there. It was as though he was made of smoke, and part of him was missing.

Matahdou called out, "Brother, it is very lonely where I am now. The healing powers have made me the keeper of the door to the land of souls, but there is no one there, and I am all alone."

Maushop said, "I guess it is time for us to consider the question of death in the world. We will have a council here, but you should go back to that other place now." So Maushop called everyone together. In those days all the animals and human beings lived together as on family, and all spoke the same language.

Maushop spoke to them all and said, "You all must have noticed how the family of Mother Earth is growing very quickly. That is because you have all been having many babies, and your babies have grown up to have many more babies, and they have grown to have many more babies, so as the generations have gone on the world is starting to fill up. Just now there is plenty of room and enough food for everyone, but as we go on bringing more and more into the world and not sending anyone away, after a while there won't be enough room for everyone, and there won't be enough food. Plants will all be destroyed, animals will starve, and Mother Earth will suffer.

"Now I can see two possible ways to solve this problem. In one of them you could just stop having babies and just go on living with the number you are now just the way you are now forever.

"In the other way, if you wanted to keep bringing babies into the world through that door we call Birth, then we should make another door, which we could call Death, so when you have been here for a while and seen the things in this world, then you would go on through that other door and experience a different place. So there would always be a flow of new people coming through this world."

Of course they all wanted to know about that other place, but Maushop said he hadn't been there and he didn't know much about it. He said that Matahdou was there waiting and had made a star path in the sky for them to follow down to the southwest. He said they would have to leave their bodies behind for Mother Earth to make into new life, because only their spirits could enter the Land of Souls. He said that it was an important decision that they would have to make for themselves, because whatever they decided, that's how it would be for all the generations to come.

So the animals and people all went into their clans, and the clans went into male and female groups, and each group began to council about what Maushop had said.

After a little while the men's groups were all finished and when they came together they found that they were all in agreement. They had all decided that they should stop having babies so that the world wouldn't get too full and they could all just go on living as they were forever. Then they looked around and saw that the women were coming out of their councils.

The females had now made one big circle so the men all went over and peeked into the circle to see what was going on. There in the center were all these little cubs, little lion cubs, wolf cubs, bear cubs, human-being cubs and so on, all playing with one another, wrestling and biting each other's ears and pulling each other's tails, and the women were all laughing and saying things like, "Oh, look at those two over there, aren't they cute!"

Then the men all looked to the oldest clan chief and said,

"Grandfather, speak for us."

So the oldest clan chief stepped out and said, "Well, the male creatures have had their meetings and we all agree. We all think it should be like this, that we will stop having babies so the world won't fill up too much and we can go on living as we are forever… thank you very much."

There was silence for a moment, and everyone turned towards the oldest clan mother. So this grandmother stood up slowly and looked around at everyone, and then she said:

"Well, the women have had their meetings too, and they have also come to an agreement. And it's not gonna be that way, no. We have decided we want to go on having babies and bringing new little ones in through that door called Birth, and so we must have that other door called Death that we can go through after a while. But the women have asked me to tell you why we decided that.

"We have noticed that we do not know enough yet about life and about living together with each other. Especially the human beings do not know enough. We keep making the same mistakes, and then we even find new mistakes to make. But these little ones, these babies keep coming to us straight from the Creator. They are very sweet and we love them so much we don't ever want to be without our little babies opening our hearts. And the Creator must be whispering in their ears before they come because they bring us new teachings all the time.

"They see when we are making mistakes, and they let us know. They have new ideas about how to do things, and they also remind us of things we have forgotten. They keep us on our toes so that we will do right for them, and not just for them, but for their children as well, and for all the unborn generations that are waiting to come here. When we understand that, then we must keep making a better world for them."

So, as you know, that was what was finally decided, because it was the women who were in charge of the door of Birth and of raising those little ones, they were the ones who had the last word. And they still do among our people, so that's how it has been ever since then.

Using my storyteller's imagination I can hear that grandmother saying to the men, "We asked ourselves what would a world be like without children? What if it were only adults, growing older, more mature, perhaps wiser, but no babies, no toddlers, no running jumping climbing shouting laughing boys and girls, no eager adolescent striving for grace and beauty through the confusions and longings of youth? What if we lived forever and never held a baby in our arms, never held a little hand as chubby legs tried to stand and walk, never had our hearts catch as our leggy young one ran a race or recited his poem in front of the whole tribe? What if, as elders, watching from the sidelines, no one came to deposit their sweet smelling babies into our arms? Where then would be the joys of all our years?

Part One

"It's not so much that we care for children because we love them, as that we love them because we care for them."

—Alison Gopnik

Chapter One
About Our Nature

"The actual state of any human being with an intelligence functioning to any extent is to love, to love, to love, to love, and being intelligent is actually the same thing as being loving."

—Harvey Jackins

That was a story from my grandfather out of our people's oral tradition. Like my grandfather I am a storyteller, and I love stories from many lands, many cultures, many traditions. Often they contain deep truths that touch our minds and hearts.

I would like to think together with you about a story from the Christian tradition as told by Matthew. You do not have to be Christian to appreciate this story. I follow my people's old traditions and am not a Christian, but the story has a lot of deep truth for me. We do not call our spiritual practices a religion. They are a way of life, a way that is based on more than survival, more than the material, getting and spending. It is based on love of life, love of the Earth and all creatures, love of children, family, friends and neighbors – not a religion but a way of spirit. I honor the wisdom found in other religions and respect those who follow them. But if you are a Christian I ask you for now to put aside any church dogma about this story and any thought about an afterlife, and consider it just as an insight about human nature, about how we regard our relationships to children.

"He called a little child to him, and placed the child among them. And he said: 'Truly I tell you, unless you change and become like little children, you will never enter the kingdom of heaven'."

"Unless you change"

Jesus is telling people that they are mistaken in their attitude about children. To be happy, to be in harmony with the universe, the kingdom of heaven, they must change. Societies based on domination in this world, based on attitudes of superiority and power vested in a few, end up oppressing everyone but the dominators – they oppress children, as well as women, elders, poor people, and minorities of any kind. Jesus is telling the people to change their way of thinking about and acting with children. Enter that story with me for a while and let us see if we can feel Jesus' meaning.

We are sitting together there when he brings that little child among us. Think about a very small child now and just look and feel that presence that Jesus is showing us. In that presence we are awed by the innocence of the child; in her we feel a pervasive sense of pure goodness. Being received by Jesus with love and respect the child is content, without fear, looking at us with a benign curiosity. It seems she wants to take us in, to absorb this whole experience, and she gazes into our eyes as if expecting a connection, connecting with another being like herself, the chance of communicating with another mind, of feeling the pleasure and acceptance of another heart.

This child accepts her life, the world about her, with interest to learn about it, with confidence to be at home in it, with joy to play with it. She laughs. It is all wonderful and exciting. We are all part of her great adventure. The child looks around at us and then back to Jesus, the one who brought her here. He smiles at her with his infinite love and understanding and she laughs again. She knows she is safe with family, with people who care about her. There is no need for a commandment. The child is the sermon. Creation has given her to us to satisfy the need we all have to give our love. And she has come to give us love and show the pure beauty of life and of all Creation.

Our children are the best lessons, the best reminders that love is our center, our essence, our meaning and our joy.

Besides the worries around keeping our children protected, fed and warm, and preparing them for life beyond the home, we still have all our other cares about family and relationships, our health and work, paying the bills, being responsible citizens. If you are a parent you know well how much you have had to sacrifice of your personal pleasures, your rest and relaxation, your energy and your time. I hope there have been plenty of moments when you were very aware that it is worth it all. Possibly there are few if any to congratulate you for your devotion, so I hope you are able to recognize it and congratulate yourself. I certainly honor and congratulate you for that dedication.

Those of you who are parents are always doing the very best you can for your children. I know you love your children and want to help them avoid the heartaches, hardships and struggles you have had to endure.

But what about this "joy" business? How much joy is there in colicky babies screaming through the night? In changing loaded diapers, trying to get porridge into an angry child, stopping everything to rush a child to the emergency clinic who has fallen and rammed a lollypop stick down her throat, stopping one from clobbering his little brother with a hockey stick, searching through panic-filled hours for a lost tricyclist, waiting with dire thoughts while staying up for a teenager out on her first date way beyond curfew?

Well, yes, that's all part of it, sure. And it is so important, this business of raising children. In fact, what in this world is more important for human beings? Not that you are likely to get very much recognition or support for it. It is the absolutely highest vocation on this planet and for it teachers and caregivers are astoundingly underpaid, and parents, who do most of the work and are most responsible, are not paid at all! Society tells you those children are your responsibility, and if it disagrees with how you perform, instead of helping you it will take the children from you. Parents are the last oppressed group to be liberated – we need a movement! (See Chapter Eleven.)

Every parent should be supported and assisted and lauded (with more than a greeting card and flowers on Mother's or Father's Day once a year) by the whole community, by the state and the nation. Every teacher and child-care giver should get better salaries and bonuses than the executives of the giant corporations, whose contributions to human society are insignificant by comparison.

There are thrilling moments perhaps to offset the parental toil:

praise of your child from a stranger, your offspring's sympathy when you are sad, prizes she has won, laughing together at a cartoon film, the older sibling proudly asserting to his school that his little brother should be accepted in the school a year early, watching your sharp young daughter stand up for herself against dumb adultist chauvinism. But the day-by-day can be wearying. Not really brimful of joy.

Joy. Joy, to me, is being fully alive in the moment, fully aware. For traditional native people, such as the elders who taught me, the way of awareness is in thanksgiving, which is why all our prayers are for giving thanks, thanks for the whole universe, for life with all its confusions and messiness, for the beauty and joy our hearts embrace, and which are continually regenerated by our children.

Thanksgiving, appreciation, fully conscious but with our awareness not centered on ourselves, so engaged we are, at one with the environment and all that is happening there – what is known in sports as "in the zone." That's the place we can be with a child. Little babies are totally engaged with the environment, playing with it, learning from it, totally in the moment. When we are with them, connecting deeply, they can take us there with them. And as they grow and learn we can take that journey again that we also took long ago and have forgotten. They open the doors to explore new worlds, and we can explore them together.

I have often been walking with three-year olds. No longer toddlers learning to master their bodies, their interests not centered on themselves but on the wonders of the world around them. With them one must be very patient, for they will stop often to investigate the wonders that present themselves at every moment. Suddenly I become aware that the little one is not beside me – she has stopped and stooped by a puddle in the path to my house. So I go back and stoop there beside her. She reaches for shiny pebbles of different colors in the water. How beautiful they are! I had walked right on by, not paying attention, intent on my goal of getting home. But she is not thinking of home, she is here, now, absorbing incredible wonders, taking them all in, making them part of her. She holds some up for me to see. She wants to share this fantastic discovery, she wants me to validate it for her and be part of this great moment with her. There is deep joy there – for both of us, in that sharing, that world, that moment, that without her I would have missed.

I want this book to be about that joy, and though I realize there is also, inevitably, hurt and pain, grief and frustration and confusion in this relationship with our children, I understand and accept them as part of that joy.

When two people are involved in a relationship deeply, each one has a natural consideration for the other as well as, of course, a concern for her-or-himself. The criterion of a good relationship is that every member derives benefit from it. And as the relationship continues and grows deeper there is a third consideration that may become even stronger than the consideration for self: consideration for the relationship. The relationship itself has a spirit which becomes important to each of them. This is the kind of relationship which we adults are privileged to be able to develop with any child with whom we spend time however briefly, if we truly connect and pay attention – to the child and to the relationship.

Sobonfu Somé, an elder of the Dagara people of West Africa, says that everything has a spirit and partakes in the spirit of Creation, and that when two people come together in a relationship among her people, they take time to enclose themselves in a sacred space and open themselves up to the spirit to guide them. Since everything in Creation is in relationship, it might be a good idea for us to consider such a ceremony for all our relationships. To begin with, here for this book, perhaps we might consider the spirit in every one of our relationships with children.

At first that would be between the newborn and the mother, usually a very natural occurrence but the more we take time to think about that, perhaps enclose that relationship privately in its own sacred space and invoke the spirit of that sacred and precious relationship to guide it, the more consciously we do that the stronger it will be.

This newborn has come from an act, hopefully of love, in a

relationship which also would be well served by being opened to spirit in the same way. There are many babies being born out of relationships that are not supportive, perhaps not existent any more, and of course that is not the optimum situation for the child or the mother. So it would be best to be very conscious and protective of this sacred act and be sure the relationship is a very conscious one that is open to be guided by the spirit that looks out for both of them and for the baby when it comes.

That optimum is not always available, but mothers struggle and manage well anyway out of the great love that is engendered for the child. One of my teachers once asked me for my early history because he wanted to know how I had escaped the oppressions of culture, of racism and classism and a broken home. The answer is my mother. She closed the door on a relationship with my addictively philandering father before I was born, and for the next six years until she found another husband and a good step-father for me, she gave me all her attention and her love, encouraging me in all I attempted, being pleased with me and telling me that I could do anything I chose in this world. She gave me the confidence to believe in myself, that what I chose I could do well and always improve and learn to do it better.

My mother did things with me, took me places, read to me and listened to me with interest and respect for my thinking. We discussed and argued and laughed and played in a world that was ours together. For those most important first six years she was my mirror and my window to the world. I am aware that it was her love, the deep quality of our relationship all through her life, with me every step of my journey, that helped me find myself in love with life, with the world, to fall in love with everyone I meet, and to stay close to children to keep me young and alive.

Love and Our Need to Give

We all need love. When we don't feel loved we long for it. But we have an even greater need to give our love to others.

So let us think now for a while about love. Love. Capital L, Love. That's what it's all about, right? The most overwhelming, most glorious, grandest moments of our lives. And the most painful, devastating, self-destructive, soul-annihilating moments too. It can take us to Paradise, as it did Dante, or dump us in hell, as it did Othello. I'd say it's the most important thing about us, but we don't understand it well. We don't investigate and examine it: where it comes from, how to diagnose and fix it when it goes wrong. And when it's not going well, most of us tend to do just the wrong things and make it worse. Pain can be a good teacher, so sometimes we learn a bit and start to handle it better. By the time we get to old age we may think, "If I only knew then what I know now!"

Before we talk about children and parents and care-givers, I think it's essential to understand love as well as we can. Where does it come from? It is present in the higher consciousness animals. I see it in wolves and dogs, whales and dolphins, apes and monkeys, for instance. Maybe the bee loves its queen, the butterfly its flower, the lizard its rock in the sun – I don't know. But there is a tenderness which caring mammal mothers show for their babies that is beyond all others.

That's where love starts for us human beings as well. Soon after the onset of pregnancy our females are taken by a sense of contentment and joy and strive to protect the embryo and wrap it in peace and calm and well-being. That is, when the mother is safe herself in a warm and supportive environment. In our stressful, uncaring society too many women and girls become pregnant in unsafe conditions of violence, drugs, abandonment and neglect, and the natural love of mother and child gets lost or compromised, twisted in anger, repulsion and fear.

That's not the fault of love or of nature. It's a fault of society, of culture constructed of pain and human ignorance only. In the natural setting of a safe nest and adequate nourishment, the love of the mother for her unborn baby grows within her as her baby grows. She attends to every movement, wonders how it is and how it will be for her child. And when the child is born the natural thing is for the baby to rest on her mother, feeling the sensations of skin, the warmth, the smell, the familiar sound of mother's heartbeat. The love of the mother envelops the baby and they are falling in love together. This is the moment of joy on which the child's growth will be based, and the establishing of a relationship that will sustain the child and guide her in all her future relationships.

It is that love, a mirror in which the child will regard herself, providing and re-enforcing her own natural love of herself, that will allow her to care for her body and keep it strong, care for her mind and keep it awake and interested, care for her heart and nurture it in compassion and joy in all life, and care for the experience of her intuition or soul that speaks to her of things beyond the range of our other senses, beyond the material, beyond rational knowledge, that tell of her place in the universe.

In that love the child will grow and prosper, and also so will the mother. In providing safety and freedom, attention and caring she will be giving the child optimum conditions for becoming the most she can be. And the mother will also grow in this relationship and will be continually learning from the child – unless she has accepted the culture's mistaken direction that the child knows nothing and must be conditioned and taught by adults.

If you are a parent, dear reader, I know you love your child very much. I hope there are also non-parents reading this book, to support all parents and children everywhere, and help them in the desire they will have to make their lives and the world better and better. Probably all of you who have opportunities to relate to children in your lives and work sometimes feel the nourishing that the love of a child can give to us. I am hoping that teachers will read this, and doctors and nurses, counselors in schools and camps, sports coaches, baby-sitters, social workers, and caregivers everywhere. I hope that everyone reading this will understand that when we have put the children foremost in our hearts, in our thoughts, in our attention and how we spend our precious moments life will be better for us, for all of us for you and for me, for the children of course, but also for our families and communities, for society, for the future, for evolution, and for the Earth.

Every year for some years now, I have had the great privilege of spending a day at a Waldorf kindergarten in Mölln, Germany. I look forward to that with a pleasure I savor in anticipation to the joy I know waits for me. There are three classes there, attended by wonderfully loving and caring teachers (I tell them I think they have the best job in this world!). As soon as I enter the grounds, the children stop their play and begin to shout my name in excitement – "Manitonquat!" I observe and enter into their play where I can, and have lunch with all of them, and later tell stories in one of the tipis they have permanently erected on the grounds. They are entranced – of course, all children love stories (don't you?). But what stays with me most when I have gone away are the memories of times when some of them may come up to me, alone or in little groups, and just stare at me silently, and in those moments I feel hit by a blow of such pure and uncomplicated love that it staggers me. It is the same in every camp we make, every school we go to, reminding me not only that these are our children, yours and mine, but they are us, their simple, open, unafraid, and unlimited love is who we all are.

Circle Way Philosophy

I have begun with the topic of love because I know that if you are a parent, love is the essence of that relationship. Your children love you, you love your children above all else. And if you are involved with children in another role, as a family member, a care giver, a teacher, a counselor, a nurse or doctor, or in any way at all, what you derive from watching, listening, and being with children is love.

As Alice Miller says, "…the stimulus indispensable for developing the capacity for empathy…is the experience of loving care."

This book is mainly about the best and most effective expression of that love. From that proceeds the joy, as well as from the exuberant joy of children who are loved for themselves, and the delight in watching them developing themselves.

For people of the Circle Way, people of the old traditions of tribes and clans and villages, the word love is not spoken often. It need not be, because it is in how they act. The word you will hear more is spirit. But it is the same thing. I did not speak of spirit right away because that is used in many ways, and often people are either confused or repelled by it.

These words, which we don't understand very well, are only sounds we make to refer to something we sense as a universal quality or force of attraction that exists throughout Creation. It binds the quanta in atoms, the atoms in molecules, the molecules in living cells. We feel in our cells that urge to connect, to come close, to cooperate, and to bind in larger entities. We want to belong and to be accepted. We bind in families, communities, nations, we bind with other species of life and with our Earth, which is binding with our sun, which is binding with our galaxy, and so on through the universe – and perhaps our universe with others beyond our ken. Some call that force spirit and some call it love.

Since you are reading this, you are educated, probably in a school, and you have not learned there about the slowly acquired wisdom of the millennia that made us all human in the first place. The wisdom human societies gained by living in close-knit circles for tens of thousands of years.

What Made Us Human

What made us human was caring for children. Caring for our babies together, being loved by them, feeling our own love and tenderness for them, their innocence and goodness, and cooperating to protect, to open new vistas for them, and in turn to be inspired by them.

What is our human nature? Our culture carries a message from ancient times that human beings are born sinful, which includes selfish, cruel, dominating and greedy. I disagree with that old estimate

– mainly because it is not helpful. I also don't think it is true. I am sure those qualities were not there at birth but were conditioned by later hurts and fear.

But I don't want to argue over truth. For me effectiveness is the measure of truth, and that old attitude is not helpful, not effective in making life better for humanity on this planet. I believe (and I see confirmation in all the newborn babies I have met, and they are many) that babies are born loving – that first love affair with their mother began in the womb, and if nothing happens to break that bond, that can be the greatest love which sets the standard for all relationships in life.

When babies are born they expect the world to be a good place for them, and they are excited and happy to be here. They look for connection, to be held and cuddled and given attention and all they need, not only physically but also emotionally and intellectually – closeness, acceptance, appreciation, and the opportunity to learn – they are endlessly curious.

They also love to play. They make a toy out of anything and a game of every activity. Fun and laughter are built in. They are cooperative, caring, and compassionate, and their love (unless it is betrayed) extends to all who come lovingly, showing themselves to be caring and trustworthy.

In a recent family workshop a two-year old boy responded to the crying of a six-month old baby, running to it, caressing its head tenderly, then running to fetch a baby bottle of water for it. No one had taught that little boy to do that. That was a natural instinct that we all have from birth. We are born, all of us, caring and compassionate.

Those qualities have been built in to our human nature through the millennia of living in cooperative egalitarian circles where everyone knew each other from birth and babies were the center of the community, the center of life, a center infused with the daring and tenderness, the play and the joy, the curiosity and aliveness of the little children.

Even today the attitudes remain throughout most of the world that, while they should be physically protected and cared for, babies must be dominated mentally, emotionally, and spiritually in order to become fully and adequately human. Adults still have the control and domination belief: that because a child is small and weak it does not know how to be a good human being. It must be educated, trained, disciplined, taught and conditioned to become like the adult masters.

That, I argue, is a deeply false idea serving only to perpetuate the mess we have made of this world.

Tribal Anthropology

My late dear friend, teacher, and partner in our native prison programs, Slow Turtle, used to jibe mainstream white audiences playfully saying, "I am an anthropologist from our people. You come to study us, but we are studying you. Because we don't understand you. I'm still looking for human beings. I think you must have been human at one time. I want to know what happened to you."

I have often felt the same. So I too have been studying anthropology. And I think I see where most anthropologists misunderstand prehistory. At the inception of human-being times people were all tribal, and in fact it was that experience of living closely in a circle of equals protecting and taking care of each other, in which our ancestors had to learn to cooperate, to communicate and work closely together, that gave us language and led eventually to the ability to plan and think abstractly, making us human. This experience developed over millions of years and we count the existence of homo sapiens sapiens for perhaps a hundred thousand years. A hundred thousand years, in which people lived together cooperatively, caring for the children, the elderly and infirm, protecting and supporting each other. Thinking as a clan or a village or a tribe. One-for-all and all-for-one. That was the very different way of thinking we had for most of those hundred thousand years.

When I began to read and listen to how anthropologists interpreted what they discovered I realized what was wrong. Those anthropologists were not tribal people. They did not think like tribal people. They described ancient peoples before civilization as though they were the individualists of today, fearful and violent competitors. Men that brutalized women and children. Men who, as they grew in numbers, had to create institutions of law and enforcement to protect themselves.

Confused by the inhumanity of civilization, I asked elders of our First Nations all over North America, "What is wrong with human beings? Why are they so inhuman, so violent, so selfish, so greedy, so indifferent to others' suffering?" The answer, in one form or another, was given to me: "They have forgotten their instructions."

The first instruction I heard about from them was always respect. Since the invasion of the Europeans people are no longer respecting the Earth, no longer respecting our relatives the other living beings, or each other. Men do not respect themselves, their own bodies, their minds and hearts that were given to them, and they do not respect women, their elders, or their children. In our old circles all were respected.

The second instruction I learned about was that human beings should live together in circles. That way they could care for one another and support one another to have better lives. In a circle all are equally important, and everyone must be heard and honored.

The third instruction I heard was thanksgiving. To live a good and happy life we must always appreciate what we have been given, give thanks and celebrate together.

I have seen the remnants of these old ways in many traditional communities, and I have been impressed by how well they still work when, in spite of all adversity, some have been able to hold to these ways. I think our ancestors – yours as well as mine – experienced those ways in the closeness, cooperation, and sharing of their ancient circles. I think they experienced both joy and tenderness in caring for their children and for their elders together.

I will not here go into why it was that these old ways did not survive into the civilizations upon which the modern world was built. That is a subject for a whole other book I may write if I live long enough. For me it was only important to find in my travels that those old ways had survived for our indigenous people of North America, at least the ones I knew about – in what we call Turtle Island, the part we now call America and Canada. There was a similarity in what I heard from elders in those places, people whose elders had themselves been brought up in those old ways.

In researching agreements among various peoples while I traveled with the North American Spiritual Unity Movement I found most often an agreement about traditional child caring. The first agreement, about the instruction of respect, was absolutely universal. I always heard from the first that the old ways taught everyone to respect the children and each other, and by being respected and seeing the adults respecting others the children learned to respect themselves and all of life. I heard usually that children could always find a place in any circle and would always be heard with great interest and encouragement from all the adults. Children were also the first to be fed, followed by the elders, although most often the children at a certain age of awareness would on their own wish defer to elders to go before them. Thanksgiving was the way in which every event and every gathering began: thanks for the Earth, for all our plant and animal relatives, for the water and the winds, for our families and clans and tribes, for all humankind and for the beings beyond in the great circle of the universe, our distant and unknown relatives, and for the Great Mystery that conferred the great gift of life.

When questioned further, during my work with the Mohawk Journal *Akwesasne Notes,* the mothers of traditional families told me that they never punished their children. Not just corporal punishment, but no kind of treatment was used that conferred the idea that the child needed to suffer because he or she was bad. Nor was any reward for doing right or well ever offered, other than the simple acknowledgement that what the child had done was noted and appreciated. The idea being that of course the child was good and smart and honest and brave and did not need to be commended for doing what was in his or her nature.

Sometimes when a child did something well there could be a special acknowledgement in a ceremony that would show that the child was beloved by all the people. That acceptance made everyone happy. If the child was experiencing problems, was confused or acting in any way not good for the community, that might be a time when an auntie, a grandparent, a clan mother or clan uncle would be able to step in to help, to listen to feelings and understand and to explain the ways of being an honorable and honored human being and member of the community.

With caring and understanding, and without shaming, children would always want to do the right thing, to cooperate and be helpful, because that was in their nature.

All Children are Our Children

I want to plant in your minds the idea that my elders held – that all children are our children, and there is nothing, no human activity more important than being at our very best, our most aware, most understanding and most caring, in our interactions with all children. I am hoping that this book will help you realize that a positive, close, understanding, and caring relationship to any child is not just good for the child, not just good for society and for human evolution, but is an amazing learning and growing and joyous experience for you as well.

There is a well-known concept that, as a teacher, in the words of Oscar Hammerstein's song, "by your pupils you'll be taught." That is, if you are paying attention to her, not trying to teach, trying to impress upon her your agenda of matter you think she must learn, but listening and staying open to learning from her. The child knows innately the most important things about her environment, about relationship, about learning and growing and just the right time to take in what they need when they need it. We all knew that when we first came into the world, but forgot as the culture, through our parents, taught and conditioned us.

Like the adults they will become, children are all different, but there are several things they have in common at birth. They do not need to be taught how to learn, or to want to learn. They are immensely curious and engage themselves totally in the environment. You can see the amazement and then the delight in each new thing they discover. They watch, and listen, then seek to touch and feel, manipulate, taste, smell. They learn, like little scientists, by experimenting and by playing. So they will learn from you – but we must be very attentive and aware of the spirit – of our attitude in the exchange. If we try to teach them we may actually interfere with their learning. If we stop it from being fun, for instance. If we bring our own needs and agenda into her process. When we give her the freedom to explore and make her own discoveries she will assimilate them faster and better. In a spirit of play and relaxed enjoyment they are very open to learn, but when we become too serious, too stern or critical of their learning, it will introduce a blockage, a disconnect in that joyous communication. When they become anxious their minds are shifted into retreat, protection, defense, shutdown and cover-up.

That's what is wrong with schools, as A.S. Neill and John Holt told us. Holt used to say that if we tried to teach babies to talk the way we teach them to read, it would be years before they really learned (and they would probably hate to talk even then). "When we make a child afraid," Holt taught, "we stop learning dead in its tracks."

Babies teach themselves to talk. The faculty of language is inherent, bred into our evolution. As with all learning, we can inhibit it by being critical or judgmental, putting pressure on them to do it our way. They learn by listening, watching our mouths and facial expressions, and imitating, playing with their sounds and movements. We can assist by encouraging, playing with them, and praising. We can laugh with them and keep it fun.

I helped my firstborn son to read because he demanded it. At two years old Tokeem was not content only to be read to. He wanted to know how those marks on the page became sounds in my mouth. So we played games with letters and words and sounds. I made cards and put them around the room and we took turns finding the different sounds and words. Because he was so eager and proud to learn and it was always fun he was reading for himself before he was three.

But our younger son, Tashin, who also loved stories, as every child does, only wanted to listen to them. Perhaps he was more interested in the images they created in his mind and the thoughts that emanated from them. We followed his lead, read and told him stories, and he learned to read much later, in his own time. But he created his own stories, asking many questions of us and of the world.

In their early years our sons were both home-schooled by our community. Each person shared his or her own interests with the boys, with all the children of the community, who explored further the things they found interesting and fun. Our sons continued to follow their interests through high school and university and today, in their thirties, they still read widely and explore and expand into new territories of knowledge. Like their parents they will continue as students and scholars all their lives.

Well now, I started talking about love and that led to talking about fun and play. I hope you got that connection, because it is important. Children are not always fun for us. They can be exhausting, demanding, annoying. They can have their own problems that cause them distress, bringing out frustration and anger. We don't love them less at those times, but it is not easy for us to express that love at that time. We often tend to express our own irritation, impatience, and frustration.

Now I know you don't want that directed at your child – at any child. They are definitely not ready to handle your problems, and that's not their job. They are your problems, not theirs. Your feelings come from many events in your own life, but not really from your children. With what they have learned and how they are feeling they are doing the best they can to handle the problems you are giving them!

Luckily, just in time for you, we have begun to get all that figured out. You don't have to dump on your children your anger or your fear or any other feelings that hurt and overwhelm you. Nor on your partner, nor your mother, nor anyone else who could get confused and hurt by them.

You do need understanding and support. Being responsible for a child is huge, scary, exhausting. It's really hard to do that alone. And you don't have to. I know what a wonderful and loving parent, grandparent, teacher, counselor, gym coach, daycare helper, scout-or-camp guide you must be. We all want to bring our very best awareness to these precious beings in our trust. I am sure you have been doing the best you know how for them. And if you are like most of us, you also wish you could do a lot better. I think we need to realize that the old attitudes of our cultural conditioning are not serving us well for that, and not serving our children as well as they deserve.

To illustrate: I watched a sweet family film on the airplane a couple of weeks ago, and the mother, a very loving, caring woman who wants the best for her twelve year old son, and his teacher, who is dedicated in his job of instructing young people and giving them a good education, each get upset by the boy cutting his class regularly to take care of a sick animal. They speak sharply to him, showing no desire to listen to the boy's feelings or ideas, only to lay down the law. I imagine almost everyone in the audience of that film did not notice that, did not think, as I did, "you would not speak to a friend in those tones, you would not so disrespect any grown human person." At least I hope not. But it seems perfectly normal for an adult to speak to a child that way. Being intelligent and caring people, when the mother and the teacher really found out about what the boy was doing, how engaged he was, how much he was learning and growing from this experience all on his own, they understood, apologized and appreciated the boy for his natural caring and devotion.

I really, really want to support every one of you now, but to do that I must give you a very different perspective from which to consider all you do and say to children.

There are things that children do not know, that we know, and it will be helpful for them to learn from us much that we have learned. They are eager to learn from us. They are also open to learn from friends, from people they trust, allies, people they feel close to whom they know have their best interests at heart.

But there are many things that children know that we adults do not – or rather that we have forgotten, because we all came into the world knowing them. If we can be open to that, open to learn from them even as we try to help and guide them, it expands us, gives us a larger view, of the world, of existence, of ourselves. Being with children in all ages, from newborn infants to…well, I don't know yet – I'm in my eighty-fifth summer and my babies are grown men from whom I continue to learn. I have many spiritual grandchildren in many countries. I have been watching and listening to the children playing and conversing with them, entering the doors they open to me, the doors into their worlds where I find the enchantment, the deep delight that justifies the title of this book.

Of course it is not easy always. It is often demanding, frustrating, disturbing, just plain tiring being with the abundant energies of our children – but none of those things preclude or exclude the deep joy we can experience with them. A joy that I find the most profound in human life. This book is about an attitude we can hold and a relationship we can foster that allow our insight and participation and expansion in further realms, an exploration we can truly make only with our children.

In the next chapter I want to explore some ways we can get ourselves in the best shape for this sacred relationship we may have with any and every child.

Chapter Two
About You, The Adult

"...you and I... are also completely good and sacred beings, all of us equally wonderful and important parts of the whole of Creation."

–Manitonquat

The Circle Way looks back to the respect and the closeness of our traditional extended families and tribal villages. My elders believed the way of the circle to be part of the Original Instructions. I have written a whole book about what I have learned about those instructions, but basically they are the way of respect and appreciation and responsibility for all beings in Creation. Consequently I believe that the original human beings a million or so years ago were guided, by the necessities of survival, to come together, to cooperate and help each other, and in doing so needed better communication, fashioning language which led to our becoming modern humans. So you may think of these instructions as your own, since your ancestors were at one time tribal people. But because so few today were actually raised in those old traditions, we have much to learn to get back to those ways of closeness, cooperation, equality, and sharing.

When I learned the practice of what I call Supportive Listening, taught as co-counseling by the international Re-evaluation Counseling community, I realized right away what a powerful gift this could be for our people, for all people, in getting back to the way of the circle. (I use this designation in our workshops and camps because I don't want our communities and work to be confused with the international community of Re-evaluation Counseling that devised and uses the term.)

Being separated and apart for so long, we do not have such closeness to a community from birth to death and are missing the trust and support needed to guide us and our children through the complexities of relationships and human emotions.

Supportive Listening fits immediately and elegantly into The

Circle Way. It proposes, as my elders did, that the universe is good, friendly to human beings, as Einstein thought, giving us challenges, but also all we need to make happy, enriching lives together with each other. When we began the Mettanokit Community we were all aware that we wanted to live tribally, as respectful equals, close to and supportive of each other. But since we had not been brought up in such a community it would present many challenges to us. And we could imagine that this practice of Supportive Listening could bring us closer, help us understand and support each other and be very good for our children. And so it proved to be.

It also turned out to be very easy to learn and to teach others, so our community was often called upon to bring workshops to other communities in our federation to give them this tool for working with their relationships, and especially with their children. Today Ellika and I use this teaching of Supportive Listening as a central tool of The Circle Way. The basics can be taught and practiced quickly and easily, and when people continue on their own, keeping to the principles of respect and confidentiality, of connecting and coming closer, not running from conflicts, but supporting, listening, understanding and appreciating each other, they keep learning from each other and making their lives and their children's lives better and better.

We are going to be thinking about our relationship to children, to make it the best we can for them and also for us. The first part of that relationship we must consider is us. You. And me. The adult side of the relationship. To be at our best for them we need to be as aware, as conscious as it is possible for us to be. The more aware and conscious of ourselves we are, the more confident we will be, the more calm and peaceable in every situation.

Listen – this chapter is important. It's about you. Don't skip over it or just assume you know all this already. Even if you do, because you are human like me you need reminders as I do. I have not found this information detailed in any other childcare book. Other books may tell you to care for yourself but they tend to lack useful details of just how to do that.

In the relentless pace of life in the twenty-first century I don't know how much time you are able to take to ask basic questions about your own nature. Perhaps, if you have a regular practice of meditation, you are quite understanding and confident of yourself – but anyway, see if what I say here fits your own thinking.

My thinking is based partly on teachings of my native elders who believed that the Creation was completely good and sacred, and that everything in it was also completely good and sacred. If you accept that, you must accept that you and I and our children are also completely good and sacred beings, all of us equally wonderful and important parts of the whole of Creation. And my thinking is also based on my own experience, as a teacher for over fifty years, as a co-creator of intentional communities and schools, as a father of two adult sons brought up in one of those communities, as one who assisted at their births and also births of other community children, who watched and listened, cared for and assisted and played with many children during their early years, including the 30 years of teaching and counseling in workshops and family camps my wife and I create every summer.

As I said above, all children are different. Every child has different experiences. (If you have siblings you may have noticed that your memories of life growing up in your family differ widely.) As children we are impressed by different things; we receive different information of the world around us. We are confused by different things, frustrated by different things, we get angry about and are hurt and saddened by different things. And we heal, if we do, in different ways, struggling to handle those things as best we can in the ways shaped by our memories and our personalities. Those confusions, frustrations and hurts are parts of the interesting differences among us.

But we are also all very much alike in very basic ways. It is helpful for us to consider those ways, because they are the heart and soul of who we are, and they allow us to interact with each other in the most positive and effective ways.

So this is about you. Who you are. Your basic nature. The nature that came with you into the world. Hardwired by evolution into your genes.

A major part of our brains – the forebrain or pre-frontal cortex, which led to language and abstract thinking and a rational capability of analyzing and understanding some of the complexities of our experiences relating to each other, only occurred after our ancestors had come together for mutual support and protection. The development of our consciousness through the human experience of caring for one another, of communicating our needs and listening to the needs of others led to some other qualities of mind beyond the purely rational.

Most importantly it led to compassion.

Compassion

It's what the Buddha taught, what Jesus meant. Our empathy and caring for the well being of others. That compassion I think of as a further development of mind, the part which people often call heart. Not that mechanical pump that brings oxygen to our cells through our blood, but our center, the place from which the energies of our total being emanate. I think of that heart, not as something in opposition to reason and the brain, but as another, later, more advanced capability of mind.

The brain developed out of the body's need to survive, as did communication and language, by which we gauge our humanness. Perhaps curiosity, which led to science, and play, which led to creativity, also began as a tool of protection but brought our consciousness far beyond mere survival.

Compassion brings another level that can even contradict the urge for individual bodily survival, as when total strangers risk their lives to enter burning buildings to rescue people utterly unknown to them.

Mother love is observable in all the more evolved mammals, and there are some, like the wolf, whose male sires may share affection for their young with the mothers and even take over the maternal caring in the absence of the female. Love for the child lasts for all the parents' lives. For us it is important that the human baby takes much longer to mature, requiring care and guidance for a dozen years or so. And that the human brain continues to grow for many years past the onset of puberty.

It is important because the small tribal communities in which our ancestors grew and became human were shaped by this relationship of closeness with and caring for children. All people of the community were part of the children's growth until their initiation to adulthood. The closeness to each child was shared by all the females of every age and affected as well all the males and the life and values of the tribe.

I speak from my personal knowledge of a large number of tribal cultures in North America, realizing that in some places in the world cultures did sometimes develop that were not egalitarian and in which women, mothers, had no authority. I believe that our societies here, in which the care of children and the power of the women as well as the honoring of the elders were central, represent the original human experience of community – the circle of equals cooperating and caring for every member.

As human beings evolved over millennia this sense of caring for little ones, of love and devotion and compassion, became part of their nature and is present today in every baby born in every culture. I often think that if they could only be treated with the same respect, appreciation, and understanding of those close-knit tribes, war would be seen now as anti-human and universally outlawed. There would be no abuse, no ill-treatment of any person in our world. We would all care for each other as our tribal ancestors did in their loyal circles, and the women, the mothers and grandmothers and aunties, would be in the place of highest honor, respected and obeyed, instead of relegated to positions of servitude and disregard. It is the mothers, after all, who show and teach the human race how to love, the primary teaching echoed in every religion.

(Note that in the history of North America, birthplace of the only cultures I know well, that there were over 500 nations here before the conquerors with their violent and acquisitive patterns came from centuries of warfare in Europe and tore the native circles apart. Despite the colonizers self-serving

versions of their histories the vast majority of the First Nations here lived in peace together before the invasion. Whenever, rarely, violence did erupt among a few, it lasted only hours, not days and months and years as elsewhere. Most nations lived completely at peace with their neighbors.)

That love affair between the mother and the child began for us in the womb, and even if it may have been broken or lost at any time, that love was there and grew from conception as an essential part of who we are now. I know you are a very loving person, even if the circumstances of your life may have sometimes made that difficult for you to realize and express. It is a basic fact of your nature. The fact is that not only do you need to be loved, you have, as we all do, an even stronger need to be able to express and show your caring to others.

There are other things I know about you, things you have in common with all babies. You were from the beginning involved with everything around you, excited to be alive, full of curiosity and energy and playfulness. You are intelligent, and able to learn quickly anything you really want to learn. When you were born you expected all to be well, and now you probably still believe that all can and will be better in your life.

I am sure you have had your troubles and struggles and trials, and I congratulate you on how well you have done, how far you have come, how hopeful you still are – as evidenced by your picking up this book, seeking to learn and grow through your caring for children. I know that at every moment of your life you have always done the very best you knew how to do at the time.

That's who you are. Yup. That's who we all are. You didn't really think you were the only one among the seven billion or so of us that was somehow left out of those blessings, the only one that must have been a mistake, the only one that there was something wrong with? So you say, what about all those mistakes I made? Well, mistakes are what we all need in order to learn. The more mistakes you make the smarter you get. Of course, sometimes we repeat the same mistakes because we didn't really get it and have to keep repeating them until we do get it.

That's because of the patterns we carry like old bad habits.

Patterns

What about all those bad habits that keep getting in our way? Whenever we are not completely present in the moment, we act out of old patterns without thought for the unique situation of that moment. When we are first hurt by others and are unable to express that to a compassionate caring person who can help us understand and heal from it, we try to figure out how to avoid those hurts when they come at us.

We try various things, running away, being aggressive, being phony, wearing a mask or a costume to hide, lying, becoming seductive in the hope of making others love us, getting furious hoping to scare others away – there are so many possible ways to try – and they might work just a little at first, so we try that again, and even if it doesn't work very well, it becomes a habit. It's what we know.

The trouble is that it keeps us from looking with fresh thoughtful consideration on every new situation, and it makes us feel inauthentic, not seen and accepted as we really are. And our automatic reactions of protection stifle our compassion for others.

Still. You are not your mask, you are not your patterns. You didn't really need those patterns when you got hurt – what you needed was to be able to express that hurt to some compassionate person who would understand and assure you of your goodness and how valuable and lovable you are, that you are a delightful, welcome, and actually necessary addition to the human race. Someone, in other words, who would reflect your reality back to you and be overjoyed that you are exactly as you are. That expression comes naturally to every baby. When something isn't right they let you know. And the healing of hurts is a natural process aided by the expression of them.

Good news. But that's the ideal situation which none of us got. As babies grow there is not always someone there to listen and help, to understand and reassure that they are safe and well, wanted and cared for. However – even better news – it's never too late for you to recover your full self. It's never too late to express those old hurts and all your feelings to another compassionate and understanding person who can remind you who you are and help you sort out and peel away those patterns that get in your way.

It's never too late to have a happy childhood.

How do you do that? Well, we learned how to be human by being close to other family and community members who cared for us, and that closeness can still work for us. Of course, everyone today is so isolated and concentrated on solving their problems alone that you will have to be the one who initiates the closeness you will need to heal the hurts of your childhood and start again to live as vibrantly and thoughtfully and happily in the present as you were meant to in the first place.

Now, since everyone in the world is facing the same basic situation as you are, trying to make life better, looking for affirmation and understanding and clarity, since everyone is absolutely good and lovable and loving, intelligent, playful, creative, wanting to be helpful and to give love, everyone around you may qualify to be that other compassionate and understanding person who can listen to your feelings and reflect back the truth about who you are and what you can do.

Look around at people you know and people you meet. They are all longing to tell their stories to someone, a therapist, or a priest, or a friend, even a hairdresser, or a bartender, or a cabdriver (sometimes strangers can seem safer than people close to you – when I was once briefly a cabdriver I heard a lot of confessions!). Because safety is the issue when we are hurt – or might be. We need to trust in the understanding and in the confidentiality between us when we let out our feelings.

Everyone wants to tell his story but no one wants to listen – or they are all trying to tell their stories at the same time. The solution? Easy. Just take turns.

Supportive Listening – Take Turns

Suggest to a friend with whom you feel some rapport that you would like to try out something that could be helpful to both of you. You only need an agreement. It only works when you agree. You both agree on confidentiality, that what you share will not go beyond the two of you. And you agree on a period of time in which one of you will listen to the other and an equal period of time in which the roles of sharing and listening will be reversed.

I call this Supportive Listening because it is different from our normal conversations. We do it because we want to help. Because everyone needs to be heard, to be understood, to be encouraged and appreciated. We all have that need, so we agree to share that Supportive Listening with each other. It's important for this that each one has an agreed upon time in which all the attention is only on the one whose turn it is to be heard.

This is different from ordinary conversation where the attentions go back and forth. With an extended and uninterrupted time the one being heard can delve deeper into feelings, their sources in their experience, sharing emotions, re-thinking and making new decisions.

The listener will be most helpful if she can put her own feelings and thoughts about herself on hold while she listens, and pay close attention to the other's feelings. If she remembers the goodness and intelligence, the caring nature and all the wonderful qualities and reminds the other person of that it will help her to be more herself and able to create a better and better life for herself and for all her relationships. If it is the listener's first experience of this process it is best if she only listens, responding only with encouraging facial expressions. Remember what the other needs is not advice or analysis, but just to be heard with understanding and compassion.

A principle goal you will have in this process is to find the places in your early memories when the patterns began that made you angry or anxious, depressed or confused and that make you feel unsure of yourself, that now get in the way of your relaxed clear, interested thinking. Find the memories of times when you were young and vulnerable, when you were not fully respected or accepted or understood, and express to your compassionate friend the feelings you had but could not then express.

I mentioned only negative feelings, as they have often the most pressing need to be released and discovering early origins for them tends to loosen their hold and helps us to find peace, clarity, and enjoyment in the present moment. But I must also hasten to assure you that happy feelings and pleasant memories can be just as valuable, often more so, in relieving yourself of old patterns of anxiety, confusion, discouragement, self-doubt, or whatever may get in the way of your clarity and your power.

Seeking to Be Free

As an example, let me share with you the first really huge breakthrough I had personally in my early working with this process over thirty years ago. My counselor in that session was a powerful leader of men's liberation, and I greatly admired his wisdom, his clarity, his empathy, and his understanding of how we all struggle under society's burden of sexism. At the beginning of the session he asked me, "Can you remember any time in your life when you felt completely free?" I thought about that and quickly scanned my memories of childhood

And there it was.

I remembered being four years old, exploring by myself away from the summer crowds at the shore, having climbed back into the great sand dunes behind the beach all alone. A skinny little dark-haired boy tanned a walnut brown through long sunny days by the sea. I had taken off my wet soggy bathing suit and was running through the hills and valleys of the sand dunes, feeling connected to the sun and the hot sand, the breeze that caressed my naked body and bowed the grasses, to the sea gulls soaring and swooping over me, the muffled song of the distant waves of the sea behind me and the infinite blue of the sky above.

Connected.

And free!

I was weeping now, weeping as I had seldom wept since childhood. Because I realized that running boy, so free and connected, was me! I must have wept for many minutes, though it felt like hours at the time. Me! That's who I was and am – I could feel it all again – the boy who was me, who had been lost, hidden from sight all those years! That vision suddenly peeled away all my protections, my pretensions, my poses, my excuses that I did not need and would never need. Because I knew now I didn't have to explain to anyone, not even to my own mind, how good, how lovable and perfect, how beautiful I am in this beautiful world. What a gift to be alive in all this beauty! How right it was that I should be here and part of it all!

Since that time, although I have had to continue to work to loosen and undo the many patterns that I had acquired over the years, I always have had that knowledge inside me to work with. I know those patterns were only old hurts that needed to be understood and healed, and that they in no way marked or stained the true me. I had and have still that naked little brown boy running free and connected through the dunes.

With a friendly, trusted and concerned friend who agrees to listen and share in this way with you, you can also re-visit your childhood and all your earliest memories, happy or otherwise, feel and express those old feelings, find some understanding and relief from them, find yourself there – that excited, joyful, curious, fun-loving and caring little person you were, and under the confusions of the old hurts still are.

The forces that created those hurts were not understandable to the little child you were then, and their authority could not be confronted. So you had to submit, give up the fight to be yourself and take on another persona in order to survive. But now you can go back to your childhood in memory, feel those old feelings as you did then, and tell your friend how it was. Maybe take your friend's hand and go back there together. With that support you can confront those old forces that gave you a false idea of who you are and could be.

Alice Miller says the children should have the right and the chance "to be accompanied on the journey to their feelings so that they could find the *correct* explanation for their feelings on their own."

(Note: what Alice Miller calls a "conscious", "knowing," or "enlightened witness" corresponds directly to what Re-Evaluation Counseling calls a "co-counselor" and to what The Circle Way calls a "Supportive Listener," an understanding and caring friend that not only every child but every adult should have.)

With the encouragement of that Supportive Listener you can stand up for yourself and tell those forces that they were wrong, that they will have no more control over your life. Whispering it, shouting it, crying through it, but standing up for yourself, proud of yourself and your life. Just feeling it will be good, but action is better – you need to make a resolution, a commitment, a promise to yourself that you will never submit to being any less than your full self. It is a promise you may have to keep making to remind yourself, but it will keep you strong and more confident in all situations. And there will be times with children when they will try your confidence and your calm and thoughtful thinking.

It's not an instant-fix. Like everything worthwhile you achieve you have to work at it. It takes time and commitment, but I assure you it does work if you stick with it, and better and better the more you do it. We all have experienced how much better we feel after "a good cry" and need ways sometimes to just "let off steam." You can arrange that for yourself just by making an agreement with a friend to exchange times of Supportive Listening. You can just decide to listen with caring but without advice or interruption to someone who is distressed, and you can even get strangers to listen to you in a pinch.

A woman told me she had gone to the airport to say goodbye to friends, and after they left she felt full of emotions and went into the café where there were many people but only one man alone at one table. She asked him if he would mind listening to her for five minutes. He said okay, so she sat down at his table, punched in five minutes on her timer, and then burst into tears. He watched amazed as she cried until the alarm sounded and she wiped away her tears, smiled, and said, "Thank you so much. I really needed that. And now I can listen to you for five minutes."

The man said that was amazing, and he saw that it obviously did her much good because she was now shining contentedly. He said he was glad that she was smiling at him now, because he had begun to worry that everyone in the café was thinking he was making her cry!

This process of Supportive Listening is based on co-counseling, and I have been a teacher of that for over thirty years. That process was put together by many people over the past six decades, inspired by the thinking and practice of Harvey Jackins, who became my good friend and supporter, urging me to go forth and create my own movement for world change. I endeavor to keep close to that process and up-to-date, as a member of a co-counseling community, finding no need to "re-invent the wheel." If you would like to learn and explore it further you can view the web site of the original international community, Re-evaluation Counseling, at www.rc.org.

I teach this tool in all my work, in family camps and workshops, and in the circles we offer in the prisons. I teach it because it fits perfectly the teachings of our elders about the circle and the goodness of all Creation and is the most effective tool I have found and also the easiest to teach. I tell you about it here because I know that in your relationship with children you want to be at your best, your most thoughtful self, communicating with compassion from your true nature not your bad mood or your upset.

It is particularly useful and important to take time to recall incidents and feelings you remember from your early years, and one of the greatest benefits of these excursions into the memories of your childhood is that you get to notice what was good about the treatment you received and what was wrong with it. You can realize that much of what the caregivers told you was "for your own good" was not really good for you at all. It was not the way a wonderful little child like you should be treated. You were not better for your thoughts and feelings being disrespected, or for being hurt and humiliated and made to feel wrong and bad. You can imagine how that kind of treatment might affect the children you are caring for now. It helps you understand their feelings. And you get to decide what would be better for you to do and not to do with them.

And I am sure you are aware that we all tend to bring the attitudes of how we were treated when we were children into our reactions to young people unawares. We want to be better at caring for our children than we were cared for ourselves when we were young. I'm sure you have thought about that and have made some conscious decisions – "I'll never do *that* to *my* children!"

That's the wonderful insight that writing this book has already given me, thinking about you and all the parents and care-givers and children I know – the thing that gives me the most hope for the world to get out of the poisonous traps of all our cultures. It is the clear fact that all of you are giving your children more than you ever received from the generation before you, and already these children are stronger, more free and creative, questioning and determined to find solutions, trying to understand their parents as well as themselves, and will bring so much to their relationship with their own children.

It's a process I have watched for nearly nine decades – it's natural and organic, it doesn't even need this book (although I'm sure all these good books are helping the process, and they are getting better and better as we all are learning.) But – provided we can just manage to keep the environment healthy enough that life continues – it is certainly, inevitably going to get better for those unborn generations my elders taught us to be concerned for.

I know you are doing your best, but you have a lot on your shoulders, you can get tired, you need some attention, some tender loving care yourself. By exploring your own childhood you can find a greater awareness of how your attitude may affect your children.

This is another reason why I want to motivate you in this book to expand your clan, your group of supporters, that circle that exists to help each other, to support you, listen to you, and encourage you, appreciate you, applaud you. It takes a village to raise a child. You haven't got a village? We should think about that. Together there's nothing we cannot do. So we will be addressing that further on in this book. It's got to start somewhere.

This chapter has endeavored to point the way for you to help yourself, with a little help from your friends, to be in the best possible shape, your most calm, confident, caring, and clear-thinking self to address the needs of the child – the next chapter addresses those.

"Eye contact, gentle touch, warmth in our voices, and caring words are balm for your child's being. You need a gentle listener, as well!"

–Patty Wipfler

Chapter Three

Relating to Children in General

"Children are human beings to whom respect is due, superior to us by reason of their innocence and of the greater possibilities of their future."

– Maria Montessori

I'm hoping you may have already taken time to do some of what I suggested in the last chapter – that is to remember the relationships and important experiences of your childhood with your own parents or other adults. When you consider the way that you were treated as a child you will have a better understanding of how you may tend to treat children now. The children you care for will appreciate and benefit from your choice to stay calm and thoughtful, to have a manner that is gentle and understanding of how they are experiencing their lives and their times with you. It will help you to recall how you felt at the age of the child you wish to relate to.

Now we move on to consider your relationship with each child, and with all children you may encounter. The absolutely best base of our relationship and attitude towards children is denoted in the term "unconditional love," coined and made famous by a very dear friend and teacher Ken Keyes, Jr. When we love someone without conditions they do not have to earn our love, do not have to behave as we wish or live up to any standard. We just love the person as he or she is, love without wavering or changing. Forever.

That's really easy at the start. You can't put conditions on newborns. They are just purely lovable and warm our hearts with wonder and delight. It is natural and human to love a helpless little baby. As they grow and expand into the world, it may not be so simple and automatic. Exploring, adventuring, testing, making mistakes, making a mess, trying our patience, being mischievous, often annoying, sometimes hurtful, they can be exhausting, problematic, troublesome, maddening, even heart-breaking, and try the extent of our capacity for love.

Loving unconditionally is liberating however. We are able to get free of our demands and expectations and our 'should' and just feel our tender, joyful feelings of acceptance and bestow all that blessing on another dear soul. And when the recipient is a child, one who looks to us for understanding and guidance, the gift is all the more precious and sacred. Loving unconditionally helps us find the true depths of ourselves.

In most circumstances it is a very natural attitude for mothers. I am suggesting that it is also natural for all human beings, for all women and all men. Love is the spirit of Creation at the center of us all. When it gets lost, choked, dampened or twisted by hurt or fear, then we have lost the deepest, most powerful and essential part of ourselves. Unconditional love is pure and unadulterated love.

To be loved unconditionally is the right of all children, indeed of all human beings. If all children all over the world were loved by everyone unconditionally, those children would grow up to create a world of love instead of fear, a world without violence or greed, as we all would have what we truly need and long for.

"Your children are not your children. They are the sons and daughters of Life's longing for itself... You may house their bodies but not their souls, for their souls dwell in the house of tomorrow, which you cannot visit, not even in your dreams."
–Khalil Gibran

That's hard to manage, even though we understand the wisdom in it. Our children do belong to us, but in the sense that we all belong to each other and to life. What Gibran warns us about is being possessive and trying to direct children's lives according to our own needs and desires when all that is important are theirs – and Life's.

If you are a parent, I'm sure you love your children, and as a family member or professional caregiver I think you also probably love the ones you care for.

Unconditionally?

Well, if that may seem more difficult, I suggest you consider them when they were newborns. You wouldn't make conditions on your love for a tiny infant. You wouldn't say, "I will love you as long as you're a good baby, as long as you don't upset me or disappoint me." When we look at a little baby we never think, "Oh-oh, this one looks like a bad one, this one's going to be trouble – looks like a criminal type for sure. Anti-social. Maybe a thief. Look at those close-set eyes – furtive, probably a liar. Sly. Don't trust him."

The idea makes us laugh. Unless we are carrying a really disturbing program what we see in the infant is pure goodness, absolute innocence. This little one doesn't want to be our enemy. He or she is looking for trust, looking for connection, looking for acceptance and closeness. She looks right into your eyes, after she has gotten her own focused. It seems the baby is curious about you, are you like her? She hasn't got the concept for it yet, but it almost seems as if she wants to know, "will you be my friend? Do I get to have you in my life?" Soon the baby will start to smile, and when he recognizes your face he will smile at you, happy to see you again. You smile, make a funny face and the baby laughs. She wants to play. He wants to have fun with you.

Connection.

That's what we human beings are looking for from the beginning. Connecting with ourselves, discovering more and more about what we are, what we want, what we are capable of. Connecting with our environment, with the world around us, the trees, plants, animals, with the environment of the cosmos, our moon, our sun, the stars, the climate, the weather. But above all, our connecting with fellow human beings. We are fascinated by each other from the beginning. To touch, to observe the expressions of face and tones of voice, to share feelings, thoughts, perceptions. From the moment we arrive we open to and thrive on gentle and affectionate human touch.

My encounter with infants began over seventy years ago, when my brother Jimmy arrived in 1942, and I was thirteen. A year and three months later our sister Priscilla was born, and a year after that their father, my stepfather Jim, died of a heart attack in bed, and I had to step into the role of man of the family at fifteen. I loved my baby brother and sister very much, and the tasks of diaper changing, bathing, clothing, and helping to feed them were to me sources of learning, pleasure, and pride. At sixteen I could forego the responsibilities when my mother remarried and I acquired two teenage stepbrothers, but I continued to help whenever I could.

At Cornell University I majored in Creative Writing and also took education courses at our local teachers college. While writing plays in New York I supported myself at first as a kindergarten teacher, then after-school counselor, and later taught at a private high school. In California later I helped raise my partner's two small children, co-founding and teaching at an elementary free school, and taught at a free university, leading me to earn a master's degree in education. When I was forty-five I met Emmy Rainwalker in Arizona and quickly realized how similar our feelings were, not only wanting children, but insisting on valuing them and all children as fully human, respecting their minds as well as their feelings. Our first son came a year later and our second in 1980, when I was 50.

Emmy and I wanted a better life for our sons than the oppressively adultist society around us. We wanted to live in a community that would respect children naturally in the way we did. Finding no community that suited in that regard, we decided to build a new one with like-minded people. We invited people to a conference with a poster that read: *HAVE YOU LOST YOUR TRIBE?* (This is also the title of my last book describing the eco-village movement and the formation of that community.)

The banner in the conference room that weekend proclaimed: "*IN US WE TRUST.*" In monthly meetings over the next three years we gathered a group we called Mettanokit (Our Mother Earth) which held the same attitude about children, and which also wanted to do away with sexism, racism, ageism, classism, and other oppressions prevalent in our society. By the time our group was ready to move together and take over the conference center of Another Place in

New Hampshire, Emmy and I had operated a day care center in our home, were teaching classes in Thomas Gordon's P.E.T. (Parent Effectiveness Training) and had taken fundamentals courses in Re-evaluation Counseling.

Re-evaluation Counseling takes a strong and well thought-out stand against all oppressions and all mistreatment in the world. Our community agreed with us that it would be helpful for all of us to have that tool to work on ourselves and our relationships, and help us with our common goals. Accordingly we engaged a teacher of co-counseling to come to us once a week for a complete immersion in that practice. That turned out to be the best decision we could have made.

New children coming to our community very quickly took to the atmosphere of mutual respect, fairness, playfulness, and creativity that we tried to engender. Chuck Esser came to our community to lead family workshops as developed by co-counseling, and we expanded our understanding of this tool.

When visitors came they were naturally quite surprised at the freedom and lively presence of the children and the ease of our relations with them. They were not used to as much play as we engaged in with them, and a few were disturbed by the self-actualized confidence and power of the young people and tried to control their spontaneity and tell them how to behave. This generally struck the children as curious, somewhat amusing. Their response was something like: "What are you, some kind of adult chauvinist?" Then they might explain, "It doesn't work like that here. We listen to each other. We have to work it out together. If you like, we can teach you." Which they often did, explaining and demonstrating the steps of no-lose conflict resolution outlined by PET.

You often hear it expressed that parents should not try to be friends with their children. I understand what they mean by that, and I think they have a valid concern. We do not see our responsibility towards our friends as that of a guide or teacher. But for me, true friendship is the basis of *every* really good and intimate relationship. I have a warm friendship with my two sons, and my mother was my dearest friend for all her life. My wife is my very best friend, and I'm sure you understand that, and hope you can believe also that my sons' mother has been my close friend since we met 40 years ago.

One difference in the relationship between adults and children and friendship among adults is that we must set limits for children. Yes – but we do set limits on other adults as well. We do not allow them to mistreat anyone in our presence. If someone pollutes the water or air we all share, we need to interrupt and put a stop to that. We don't allow people to hurt themselves. When someone is drunk we take away his car keys. We restrain people from hitting each other or jumping off bridges.

When we must restrain an adult it is because he is out of control. The same is true with children. The difference is only that children have less knowledge and understanding of themselves and the world. There are times when we must intervene for their own sake as well as for ours. We do not want them to harm themselves or others or cause damage to things in our environment. And in reality neither do they, although at the time they may be unaware of that. So we interrupt the mistreatment, firmly, but in as gentle and loving and understanding a way as possible.

I will go further into the subject of setting limits for children in a separate chapter. For now I only wish to point out that there are limits to behavior that we do set for everyone in order for us to live in safety and harmony together. That doesn't mean we can't be friends. Of course we can.

Jesus told people to love their enemies. After two millennia that is still a radical concept. And yet, quite possible. My friends in the ecovillage of Tamera in Portugal have a Global Peace Institute which sponsors a Peace University in summer, it initiates peace pilgrimages and peace villages in violent areas of the world. The youth in that community have a play they present when they travel and carry a banner inscribed with its title: *We Refuse to be Enemies.*

So I would offer that it is not only possible but also desirable to be friends with our children and with all children, while maintaining our responsibility to care for them, to be a guide through the complexities of living in our time, and help them discover themselves and be the most of what they be, make the most of their lives and their challenges. A friend is someone you can trust, someone who is honest and straight with you, who tells you what he knows and thinks in a way that you can hear and understand. A friend is also someone whom you can depend on to do what he says he will do.

As a single mom in her early twenties, my mother raised me alone for the first six years of my life. We were very close, and she was what I relied on to tell me about the world. If something happened to prevent her from doing what she told me she would do she always, always apologized and found a way to make it up to me later. She could get angry with me for something I did or did not do, but I never for one moment felt that meant she did not love me, that she did not consider my wishes or that I could not trust her. I learned that, like everyone, I could not always get what I wanted, but I knew she would be sure I had what I needed.

I have heard people say that you should not be friends with children because a leader must not be friends with his followers, or a teacher with his students. I'm sorry, but I think those are just good examples of much that is wrong with this culture. In the most effective up-to-date leadership training people are encouraged to get close to the people who work with them, to listen to them, to understand their problems. People work more willingly and diligently under such leadership. The teachers who meant the most to me were those who gave me friendly interested attention, and those were the ones I learned from best and most.

Maria Montessori wrote, "education is not what the teacher gives; education is a natural process spontaneously carried out by the human individual, and is acquired not by listening to words but by experience upon the environment." She also said, "The environment itself will teach the child…without the intervention of a parent or teacher, who should remain a quiet observer of all that happens."

Personally I like the concept of friendship in all relationships, but perhaps that word seems inappropriate by your understanding. Okay. Whatever you call it, what I want is for us to relate to children with complete respect for who they are. Respect for their bodies, respect for their thinking, respect for their feelings, respect for the sacred beings that, like us, they are.

Respect for their bodies includes being sure what they ingest as sustenance or for pleasure is healthy, educating ourselves and them about that. It includes being sure they get enough rest and sleep as well as exercise, and that they have a positive attitude about their bodies and their looks. It means we need to show care and respect in the way we touch them. Friendly affectionate touching in appropriate ways is wonderful and nourishing, but not hitting, jabbing, slapping, spanking – or tickling (aggressive domination in the guise of fun).

Respect for their thinking doesn't mean we believe all their thoughts are wise and true. Some of them may be, some not, but we are happy that they are thinking and expressing them, even when we understand they need more information. It means we listen to them, we take them seriously. They are using their minds and ideas to try and make sense of the world, and that can be appreciated at any age. My mother always listened to me. From my earliest memories of being a chatty little three and four year old she took the time to hear me out and responded thoughtfully and honestly, no matter how strange, childish, or far off my ideas may have been. We had long, excited, sometimes heated arguments, and I learned a lot trying to articulate a position or propose a contrary view. I was often wrong, of course, not having enough information, but the discussions broadened my knowledge and my views – and occasionally I had a valid viewpoint which mother accepted and acknowledged. She was an intelligent and well-read woman and all her life I valued her critique of my writing. How grateful I am that when I finally published my first book at age 60 (*Return to Creation*), she, at 81, called me up, having read it at one sitting, to tell me it was wonderful! As she was a thoughtful woman, highly critical, and a lover of great literature, that testimonial I treasure above all.

Respect for their feelings means paying good attention when children are expressing emotional reactions. The discharging of their hurtful feelings may cause feelings in us that makes us want to discount their feelings and divert them from expressing them. People say things like "Oh that didn't hurt so much," "Don't be such a baby." "Stop being a drama queen." "Be a big boy – men don't cry." "That's not really important, why make such a fuss?" or we try to divert them – "Come help me make some cookies," "Let's see what's on TV," "How about some ice cream?" All of that is completely disrespectful and failing to hear or even try to understand what the child is experiencing.

Perhaps it is getting better now than when I was a boy. What I heard, not from my mother, but from many grown-ups, was "Children should be seen and not heard," "If you want to act like that, go somewhere else," "Stop crying or I'll give you something to cry about!"

When I hear a child cry, or scream, even have a full tantrum, after I ascertain that there is no physical problem that needs fixing, I am thinking to myself, "Oh, good, he is getting it out. doing what is natural and discharging a painful emotion." I am aware that the discharge is a necessary function of healing. At least a beginning.

When the child has released the pressure and been heard by an understanding, sympathetic person, sometimes that by itself is enough. That is all she needs to deal with the hurt herself. But often there is more to consider to understand the source of the hurt, and an experienced and compassionate adult can help, assuring the child how good and valuable she is, how smart and strong, how loved and appreciated she is, how sorry we are about what she has suffered, that it was in no way her fault. And that we are very glad she shares her feelings with us and we will continue to be there for her when she needs us.

I am glad when I hear a child cry.

The first thing I will do upon hearing any child cry or scream is to check to see if a responsible adult is there to assist with what may be the problem. If no one is yet on the scene, I may approach carefully to provide reassurance to the child that he is being heard and not abandoned, that mama will return and his world restored, and I will try to discover if there is a present hurt needing medical or other attention. If a parent or care giver is on hand, I will offer support and understanding, assuring her she is not alone in that difficult time, that she is doing very well in the situation, and also listen to her when the child's crisis has passed.

Whether you choose to think of the adult role as that of a good friend, as I do, or whether you may prefer another term – the essential ingredient is trust. That trust is gained by caring, by respect for the child's body, mind, heart and spirit, showing that respect by listening, indicating understanding, and by honesty, consistency and dependability. I like the term ally, because young people face such oppression in this society that I would like them to stand together with adult supporters for the freedom to be their full selves. More about the societal oppressions and being allied to young people will come in a later chapter.

So we are back to respect as our primary instruction in caring for children. That respect is the primary instruction you will find everywhere among our traditional elders. We hear it all our lives, in social gatherings and ceremonies, but the most important teaching is not ever by words or by rules. Our children respect others, if they do, because they saw the adults in their communities respecting one another. They respect women because women were respected and held very important positions in the community. They respect elders because they saw everyone treating the old people with utmost honor and reverence for their service to others in their lives. They respect little children and respect themselves because they are treated with complete respect by all the adults.

The thing about respect as an instruction is that it is something we all can do. We all *could* love each other, but that's a bit more difficult, more complicated, involving how we *feel*. It's very easy for me at eighty-five to love everyone, because I understand that their unlovable patterns are not who they are, who they want to be, and not their fault.

So I can just look past them to see the hurt little child inside and just love the whole package. But I didn't always get that. There were many that I did not and would not love when I was young. I could not love just because I chose to, because I thought I ought to and told myself to love. But I could choose and decide to completely respect everyone, even if he seemed nasty to me. Because respect is about *behavior*. You can choose your behavior, but it's a lot more work to choose your feelings.

Love, as I said, is our essence and is the way we all would naturally relate to one another if we had not ever been hurt, or if we had fully healed from all hurts and were completely present in our essential good nature. It helps to understand that if anyone does not love you and treat you well, it's not your fault, not even his fault, it's because he has hurts that never healed. Look at it like this: if he loved himself he would love you too.

Unconditional love then, is there in you now and in me, obscured sometimes by unresolved old hurts and the patterns formed by them. The connections made in the womb and at birth are so powerful for most mothers that they easily bond with their babies with a love that is completely unconditional and never ceases in their lifetimes. My plea to all of you here is to strive for this bond and to keep it intact.

At first that is fairly easy. This little person is so adorable and so helpless the whole world would love her. If the fathers stay close they too will experience this unconditional love from the beginning, and they will gladly assist all they can in the tasks of attending this helpless babe.

Humanization by Caring for Children

I am glad to hear of more and more papas who are sharing the parenting responsibilities more equitably, and thereby not only relieving the burdens of mamas, but bringing more joy into their own lives and the lives of their children. My two sons are both stay-at-home papas while the mamas go to jobs. In a number of enlightened countries like my Ellika's Sweden, the laws and industries now provide for paternity leave for men and make it possible for both men and women to be home in the important time of adjustment and provision for the baby and the whole family after the birth.

There is a net gain for everyone in this trend. There is research about men who may have been dehumanized by their isolating roles in business and industries, limited by preoccupations of financial stress, the pressures to get ahead, the ostentation of material indications of status and the cultural instruction that it is somehow unmanly to have or show any feelings except anger – when such men are required and are able to care for children they become gradually transformed. Just being in the company of and responsible for these endearing little ones, so helpless, needing nurture and attention, men become more empathic. More tender and gentle, more understanding, more able to be in touch with and express their own emotions.

If we could only manage to get all men the time, responsibility and instruction to discover the joy of caring for children, how the misplaced values of civilization would be altered, what happier generations we would raise, and what a lift the prospects of human evolution would be given!

But we must also face the situation that while many more men are discovering the joys of caring for children, at the same time a terrible percentage of families are torn apart by men abandoning mothers and children. Some pay monetary child support but little else, many just disappear. And even for those who accept a joint parenting role, the situation of part-time fathering is not enough. One parent is overworked, unable to provide the attention for the many years it takes a human child to mature. Our children, the light of our existence, deserve more from us.

They deserve our full attention in the years of their immaturity. They deserve our deep caring and understanding. They deserve the best of us, our time, our good thinking and creativity. They deserve our liveliness and joy, our craziness and fun, not an expensive education necessarily, but they deserve to know they are wanted, that they belong, that they are the greatest gift that life has given us. And that they have all they need to make their own lives as wonderful as they have made ours.

> *"That humanity which is revealed in all its intellectual splendor during the sweet and tender age of childhood should be respected with a kind of religious veneration. It is like the sun appearing at dawn or a flower beginning to bloom."*
>
> –Maria Montessori

Here I want to insert a brief digression to advise new parents about the family bed, the activity that sometimes these days has the strange name co-sleeping. There has been some controversy and argument about this, but for me it is very simple. For millions of years in the history and pre-history of humankind there were no separate bedrooms, and families naturally all bundled together in their lodges. I do not consider that a hardship due to ignorance or poverty – I consider it a hardship to have a baby in another room, in a crib, alone, without the familiar warmth and comfort of mother's body, father and siblings all happily cuddling together – a hardship for the mother and for the father. And for the baby such isolation is close to abuse.

When the separate bedrooms and beds appeared did they make the children happier, stronger? Did they strengthen the bonds of love in the family? Did they make night feeding easier for the mother? Considering the history of the last five thousand years of civilization versus the experience of traditional indigenous peoples, I would say quite the opposite on all counts.

Emmy and I both understood this, and our sons shared our family bed until they decided they wanted a bed and space of their own. In the early nursing periods it was much easier to provide immediate nighttime feeding without having to get up to the howl of a hungry infant and put on robes and go to set up where the baby slept. When Emmy and I separated after seven years the hardest thing for our boys was giving up the family bed, which they loved. Later, when Ellika came to live with us, she quickly took to the family bed and to having two small growing boys beside us. The warmth and comfort of cuddling into the dreamtime makes for a strong bonding.

Today I have a eleven-year-old grandson, who has his own bed, but many times he has preferred to cuddle with his parents. Now he gives over place in the family bed to a new baby brother. It is not an issue, but an obviously good and loving thing for all. I am happy that my new grandbaby Marla also sleeps in the loving embrace of a family bed with her mama Frieda and her papa, my younger son Tashin (they have constructed a tiny trundle attached to their bed but when she started crawling out they set it down to floor level so she would not fall from the bed when she goes exploring on her own).

Back to my theme of keeping the bond intact. This is the theme of many systems and books with names like Attachment or Connection or Natural Parenting. It is one of the reasons, besides physical health, for breast versus bottle-feeding. For the mother bonding is, as I said, quite easy with a tiny infant totally dependent on you. But in a while there will naturally come pressures that strain or break that bond. If we are able to stay aware of the child's perception and feelings we can take measures to strengthen the bond or repair it quickly in those stressful times when it may be strained or broken.

It is not the child who will first break that bond between you. The child has no concept of a bond so cannot make a choice to preserve, ignore, or break it. It is up to us as adults to be conscious of that bond and its importance in maintaining closeness and trust. Being as calm as thoughtful, as aware of the child's experience and understanding as we can, we are able to preserve that bond. When we do something unaware that does break it, we can take steps right away to repair it. If such breaks are rare and closeness re-established the bond will stay strong. The love you have for the child, and the child for you, cannot be damaged by occasional mistakes.

I think that the first time you, or any of us felt a sudden change in the flow of love, acceptance, and appreciation we were used to as a baby, it was a terrible shock. The world was not as we had believed. For some reason, not understood by us, we were not surrounded by the warm glow of delight in us. We felt abandoned, confused. The expressions on the faces and in the voices or people we loved and were dependent upon had become hard and harsh. Probably we were stunned, deeply distressed by this sudden change. When our cries of anguish brought no compassion, it must have been terrifying.

If the person causing this hurt soon understood your distress and began to comfort you and listen to your feelings, showing that they had been understood; if then when you were calm again, the person would carefully, thoughtfully explain what caused her upset, did not blame you, perhaps, I hope, even apologized, that unexpected severing of the bond between you would be healed. Children know when love is real, and they soon learn that all of us make mistakes and get upset sometimes, and they make allowances for us when they feel safe.

One reason why the bond between you should be diligently guarded, preserved and treasured, is that you both will need that trust in all the years that lay ahead. The young person needs someone with whom she will always feel safe to express her feelings, her anxieties and fears, her confusions in life's inevitable dilemmas. And you will need that information in order to understand and support her or him through confusing years of growth, school, friendships and hostilities, sex, drugs, money, and other social pressures.

"A new human being, treated with respect and kindness and receiving accurate information about the environment would start out and remain a person of integrity and a person of great courage."

–Harvey Jackins

New parents be warned: your first tests begin as the baby reaches out into the environment to discover what is there and what he can do with it. Be ready for the change, but stay calm, the change is not bad, only more interesting and deserving of some thought. He will make a huge mess, destroy what he can, create an insufferable racket, and pull on you constantly for your attention when you want to work or relax. Of course that's absolutely correct, perfectly normal, that's their job.

To grow and learn, which they do by reaching out, exploring, playing: how does it feel? Does it come apart? How does it taste? Can he eat it? How far can he throw it?

Of course you must baby-proof the environment and keep whatever may be harmful or dangerous or valuable safely away. Be sure everything baby can get at by crawling, toddling, or climbing is out of reach.

Even so the baby will find ways sometimes to drive you up the wall. Sometimes it will seem they are really working at being obnoxious, and your patience will be sorely tested. That's part of their testing the world, part of their learning. They are not trying to be mean, they are only playing – remember that's their job. They will be shocked if you get angry or upset or display impatience or displeasure with them. If they smash a treasured object they will understand if you are sad, but not if you are angry, because they did not do it to cause you grief or annoyance. Be comforting when they are sad or confused, and invite them to help you clean it up, listening to them, mirroring their feelings, and explaining your own, listening again and thanking them for their help and understanding, and for showing their feelings to you.

The closest bond would normally be between the mother and child, but all of us, fathers, siblings, grandparents, other family members, baby sisters, teachers, counselors, librarians, social workers, everyone can develop special closely bonded relationships with children, which can bring more support and more joy into their lives and into ours.

Even if you are not a parent and are available to children only for short periods, a class, or a counseling session, a sport or other activity, you can develop bonds with them. Most of them are really looking for allies, people who can be counted on reliably to help them in understanding themselves and the world. As a storyteller I feel this bond beginning every time I connect with them and tell a story. Or if I engage in playtime with them, or take them on an outing to discover something new. But first and foremost by listening to them.

Listening to them and then repeating back to them what I think they have tried to express. Mirroring, it is often called: "So, what you are telling me is…" And then showing you understand what they are experiencing and feeling, and that their feelings are fine and important to you. Showing that you are very happy and honored that they share them with you.

The language in which you convey all that will vary according to the age of the child, but it can be done at the earliest age. Even pre-verbally we can communicate all that with our eyes, facial and bodily expressions, and tone of voice. It is a communication of the heart, immediately understood.

To build this bond we need to do this often, in all connections with children. Each time we do this we are building more trust, becoming a resource with which all children love to connect.

So make this sequence automatic in reacting to children's expressions of feelings, both positive and negative:

Listen first, with interested and caring attention.

Next report to the child that you understand what they mean to communicate.

Then show that you appreciate how that feels to the child.

When your response elicits a further expression from the child, be prepared to repeat that sequence of listening, mirroring, and showing your understanding. Most often that may be enough, all that is required for the child to unload, feel understood and supported, and she will be ready to move forward with confidence in her ability to handle her situation. Sometimes the child will ask questions seeking further information and understanding, which may lead to a conversation that would be important to both of you.

In any conversation I would encourage you to adopt the attitude of an intimate friend, not a teacher. Thomas Gordon says somewhere that the first time we relate advice to a child it is information, the second time it is a lecture and subsequent repetitions will be tuned out. A trap that, even though I knew and taught it, I sometimes fell into myself. From my sons I might get a reminder verbally or with a roll of the eyes. Sometimes I would just notice their eyes glazing over, and I would ask, "Have I said this before?" And they would nod and sigh. "Only a hundred times, Pop." Perhaps I was not completely incorrigible. I keep learning and think I am a lot better now. Patience. We adults are often a little slow.

Children are smarter than we generally give them credit for. When they are not pressured or judged, they usually are tolerant of our lapses. I remember a girlfriend of my younger sister once musing when they were in their teens, "I wonder if when I have a daughter she will be as much wiser than I am wiser in relation to *my* mother."

To sum up this chapter I return to the basic influences of human behavior: love and fear. I have referred to the oppressive aspects of our cultures today. Of course, not all aspects are oppressive, only those whose origin is in fear rather than human love. No doubt today's cultures are, in the main, a considerable improvement on cultures of the past. Except in regard to that of the First Nations of America, the ones I am most familiar with, where their development was massively overturned by colonial conquest. There is now a complex interim condition of internalized oppression, but with some more hopeful efforts at a return to older traditional native values.

I do not encourage anyone to romanticize our native past, to idealize the "noble red man." Human beings are more complex than that everywhere, and the potential for violence, competition, destructiveness and hostility remains and obscures often our inherent peaceful, cooperative, creative and affectionate nature.

What is very clear to me, both from my academic studies of human history and pre-history and from my personal experience in contemporary traditional tribal life throughout North America, as well as through our circles in the prisons and the personal counseling I have done for forty years and more, is that the presence of love and trust allows us to flourish and the presence of fear and hostility corrupts individuals, nations and cultures. (There is a reason why we did not need police or prisons, courts or lawyers before the Europeans invaded.)

This puts the future of our children, and by extension the future of our entire society, in our own hands. We are the ones who can ensure that our children are surrounded, at least in the crucial first six years of their lives, with love, with an emotional environment that allows them a wide scope of confidence, self-appreciation, freedom and encouragement to explore and find the beauty and richness of life. We can reduce fear and trauma, and where it occurs inevitably we can also heal it, with listening, understanding, and the reliable medicine of compassion and love.

One of the most powerful tools we can wield in this all-important enterprise of connecting with children is play. It's going to take some learning and re-learning, but that is where we can most effectively reach children on their own turf, in their own terms. It is so important we will take the next whole chapter now to explore it.

Part Two

"The natural emotional tone of a human being is zestful enjoyment of life. The natural relationship between any two human beings is loving affection, communication and cooperation."

–Harvey Jackins

Chapter Four
Play Time

"The more intelligent the animal, the more it plays."
–Manitonquat

We generally come into this world expecting no problem. Unless we experience some severe difficulty in the womb or at birth – in such case the immediate connection with the warmth and comfort of mother's body generally will soon restore baby's sense of well being. Free of anxiety we begin to look upon what our senses reveal with wonder, then with curiosity and great interest. It soon becomes apparent that we also have a sense of fun. We begin to smile, and soon we laugh outright. As the actions that make us laugh grow in number it becomes obvious that we human beings love to laugh and we love to play.

In our old language we have no word for "work" – there are words for all our activities, but none of them was thought of as work. It was just what they were doing. If what they were doing got tiresome they would do something else for a while. When I was a child and had a job to do I always turned it into play, made a game of it somehow. As children that's how we see the world.

Once when I took my younger son to see the beaver houses in our nearby lake, I marveled at seeing six large maple trees on the ground that had been felled by sharp little teeth.

"Tashin," I said, "I wonder why the beaver would cut down these huge trees that are too big for him to move or do anything with."

Tashin observed the trees thoughtfully, then came out with a gem of four-year old wisdom.

"Maybe it was fun," he said.

The business of children is to play. That is their job. It is how they learn, about themselves, about other people, about the world. It is also how they communicate. They communicate their thoughts and their feelings to themselves and to us in play. Particularly at young ages when they are unable to articulate their experiences in words. If we pay attention we can learn much of what they are thinking and feeling by watching and engaging them in play.

So when we curtail their play we are hindering their learning. If we don't try to control their play and just encourage the child to take the lead, they will show us what they are working on, what they are trying to understand, what is important to them, and how they are feeling.

Of course there are times when we can enter in and suggest new play, especially if they seem to be stuck and demonstrating their hurts or confusions on each other. Then we can alter the attitudes by being silly, making them laugh and perhaps getting them to turn on you to use you as focus of ridicule.

Playing with children is an important part of relating to them. It gets us closer, providing fun and happy times they will treasure in memory for the rest of their lives. Playing strengthens the bond between us and them and it can also repair the bond if it becomes worn or severed.

"...play can save your life...Play is the vital essence of life."

—Stuart Brown

Playing with a child is not so easy for us adults. We are a long time away from our own childhoods. For a lot of people playing with children is either bewildering, scary, or just boring. Too bad for us, because we are missing a lot of fun, but it's not too late. Even if you have no children of your own you can always borrow some and learn from them. And it is one of the most important skills we can learn in caring for children.

Dr. Lawrence Cohen thinks so, and if you read his book *Playful Parenting* you will understand why. I am tempted to end this chapter here and just tell you to go get his book. You will get more than just a rich flavor of his playfulness – it is a complete course in caring for children of all ages, and not only for parents, but also really useful for anyone who assists or just hangs out with young people.

But this issue is so important I must try to give you at least an introduction to playing with children. As an adult you probably do not play enough yourself, and when you do it is probably the wrong kind of play – full of competition, winners and losers: "the thrill of victory and the agony of defeat." But when you get the idea you can start practicing and trying out your new playing skills with children at every opportunity. And practice makes fun.

How shall I begin? Well, one piece of good advice: be a clown. There was a Cole Porter song in *The Pirate* which Judy Garland and Gene Kelly sung and danced in floppy shoes, baggy pants and red noses: "Be a clown, be a clown, all the world loves a clown." (Well, almost all. Very young children and babies can get very scared at the weird makeup and madcap antics of circus clowns.) But even little babies laugh when we make faces at them – as long as they recognize it as play and not threatening.

Larry Cohen advises us to lose our dignity and find our children. Maybe that's hard for you. I understand. But talk to yourself. It's in a good cause. Tell yourself to loosen up. The kids will love it and love you for it. Adults are watching? So you feel embarrassed – most of the adults watching will be envious at your ability to make a fool of yourself and get laughs. The abrupt transition from your serious demeanor to utter silliness is hysterically funny to the kids.

My mother, a beautiful woman with a commanding presence, could make me helpless with uncontrollable mirth with one facial expression. Not only me, but ten years later my new brother and sister would also collapse screaming with laughter when she complied to our demands to "make a monkey face."

What comic performer made you laugh when you were a youngster? I think of Robin Williams impersonating my friend Dr. Patch Adams in that film. As a young person I was much taken by Ray Bolger as the Scarecrow in *The Wizard of Oz* and perfected his elaborately clumsy falling walk, which I still use on kids. But my real comic mentor was Danny Kaye. I studied his facial expressions when talking to children and telling stories, his vocal tricks and the travesties in his movement – see *Hans Christian Andersen, the Secret Life of Walter Mitt*, and best of all, *The Court Jester*. I memorized every song on his record, and it was a high point of my life to see and savor his one-man show at The Palace in New York. All that, plus a little Chaplin, Buster Keaton, and a touch of Dick Van Dyke, have gone into my style of playing with children as well as storytelling. You don't have to be a pro, but do think theatrically, mock opera and melodrama, ham it up, over-emote, scream, giggle, pop your eyes, fall on your face, put on exaggerated dignity as you do something totally stupid. Children feel stupid a lot – remember how it felt not to know something it seemed everyone knew? So they love to see us be hopelessly dumb. Larry's advice: "Bungle, blunder, and stumble."

If you feel yourself getting annoyed at something a child is doing, overdo being mad so that it is ridiculous, a joke on yourself – they will also get where your feelings are coming from. "I'm so angry I'm just going to put my head in the toilet!" (You don't need to do it – if that doesn't get a laugh, keep going, the more absurd the better.) As Larry says, "It takes a village idiot to raise a child."

It's wonderful to laugh together with children. They love it, we love it, it's pure joy. You can get laughs having them chase you, falling and crying for mercy, and when you chase them, almost catching them but you are too clumsy, and when they are almost in your grasp you trip and fall, and they escape screaming with laughter. As Patty Wipfler says, "Children love to play games in which they are the swift, the brave, the sure, and the adult is the slow, the timid, the befuddled."

When they get you with their ray gun or their light saber, die gloriously and slowly. Or, Larry's suggestion again, when they shoot you scream, "Oh no! It's the Love Gun! What can I do? I'm in love…can I hug you? Let me kiss your toes…please, please, please!"

"Play…shapes the brain, opens the imagination."

–Stuart Brown

Children don't get enough play. Especially when they get to school age. Even in pre-school and kindergarten we have begun to control their play. Not too wild, now! All right, calm down, quiet down! No roughhousing! News flash: Children are wild and boisterous, full of steam they must get out. Roughhousing is great for getting out energy with fun and for the comfort of safe touching – for us and them.

When we get the impulse to clamp down on children's play we should check that with suspicion. Are they unsafe, is there any real danger threatening? Or is it just too energetic, too loud, too chaotic for us? Do we want them to be nice well-behaved little mannequins? Or do we want them to be real children? Children are loud and wild sometimes, and if they can't get all that out, where is it going to go? At my age I know I'm just envious of all that energy!

If it really threatens to get out of hand and there is a possibility of injury or the fun is getting violent, we can leap in with our crazy clown or village idiot act and divert the energy. If they start to fight over a toy we can grab it and make them chase us. We can grab one of them and fall down on top of him, letting the other jump on us.

That physical touch, wrestling, hugging, rolling around on each other on a couch or the floor, establishes a connection that is good for all of us. There is a problem that the real threat of pedophilia could make us withhold the healing touch of our pure human affection from other people's children. Let's talk about that with each other. Let's make sure the environments where our children will be are guarded and are safe, and when they are let's remember how important that physical touch and healthy affection are to the emotional well-being of all children. Pats on the shoulder, tousling of hair, holding hands, pulling onto laps, hugging, snuggling, playful wrestling, all are part of the connection all of us long for.

At a recent circle a four-year-old boy with a lot of four-year-old energy solved his need for active play and for attention by racing around inside the large circle of seated participants. His boldness inspired two other boys, only slightly smaller, to join in. Round and round they went at top speed. It was fun to do, I could see, and fun to watch if you had no other agenda - like being at the races. I didn't want the fun to stop, but it was difficult to concentrate and for the circle to listen to each other. I decided the best thing to do was join it.

So I jumped up and started to run with them. They whooped with laughter at that and round and round we went, the whole circle also laughing now. Then I took the hand of the lead boy, and swung him around off the ground, set him down and let him swing me around him. Back and forth we went, every time I let him swing me I acted clumsy and goofy and stumbled around, then managed to get it together to swing him. To add to the fun, I let go his hand and spun out, falling and sprawling on the floor. Then the other boys joined in and all three jumped on me. I grabbed them and we all wrestled and rolled all around the floor – me the helpless fool, them laughing hysterically.

I crawled to my chair eventually, dragging them all, then sat and took one on my lap, but they got it that I was exhausted so all ran off to play in another room, and the circle went on with its agenda.

Go for the Laughs

Look for the laughter. Laughter releases tensions of fear, anxiety and confusion, and if you are paying attention it will give you a clue about their feelings.

It has been found that pre-schoolers laugh three to four hundred times a day. When was the last time you laughed even a hundred times in a day? Maybe at a Chaplin film festival. Every day our children are processing billions of bits of data, bombarded by new experiences, new information. Play is how they are making sense of all that.

It is fine when they play alone. That's where they are learning about themselves and how they might relate to what is coming at them in their lives. I was an only child for thirteen years, and for the greater part of that time I played by myself. I do not remember ever being lonely or being bored. Everything in the world was just too interesting. My mind and imagination were always engaged. Everything told me a story.

Very early I acquired a huge box of hand puppets, and I would entertain myself for hours with stories I made up for my people to perform. Later, at about eight, I was given a small theater with a rollup red curtain and grooved stage where I could place scenery I made myself and move lead figures about from below, putting on plays for my aunt and grandparents.

Child psychologist David Elkind, author of the book *The Power of Play,* asserts that kids prefer to play with other children, that adults are a last resort. That depends quite a bit on the age of the child of course. Playing with other children is important for developing confidence and social skills. Children usually do quite well sorting out their play with each other and learning from each other. But there are times when they may get stuck and could use some assistance from an understanding adult.

Children really love to have adults play with them, if they are really *with* them and not *against* them. We play with them so seldom that they are used to our not wanting to, and if they think we won't play, they won't ask us to. In our camps the children look forward to the periods we allot for playing with them every day – (a lot because the adults in camp are learning the things you are reading in this book.) We need to take the initiative and ask to play with them. What they don't want is for us to take over their sport as I'm afraid we often tend to do. And it doesn't help for us to show off and show them how good we are. Better to applaud how good they are.

Our attitudes toward sports have been ruined by competitiveness. The need to win and not to lose so ingrained in our competitive society. I know whenever I play tennis, I have to remind myself not to get caught in the competitive urge, but to do my best in every point and rejoice in my opponents' successes – that way I enjoy the match so much more. It's very good to play zero-sum games with children and to remind ourselves that the playing is their time, not our time.

A lot depends on the age of the child. Little children are used to feeling powerless. Everything is built for big people, the child cannot drive the car, rarely gets to choose what to do, where to go, what to eat. So when we play a game with a small one, and we can manage to lose, to him it will be a great victory! He needs to crow and be congratulated.

At a Finnish family camp years ago I gave this talk to the adults before playtime, and after a rousing afternoon of football (soccer) with both genders and all ages the men came back exhausted. It had been so much effort, mentally and emotionally, for them to refrain from cutthroat competition, to give all the littler ones chances to steal the ball from them, and to cheer enthusiastically whenever the other team kicked a score. They had to discharge a lot of old memories of sporting humiliations when young. But after that day playtime became for fun for all.

As the young people grow older and get more skilled, we will want to provide more and more resistance for them to stretch their abilities and make their victories sweeter. I readily admit to my own failings in this with my older son. Before I learned about this I taught him tennis in the hope of getting a good partner for my late return to the game of my youth. At thirteen my son Tokeem was strong and coordinated and could really slam groundstrokes. But when we played games, my overall skills allowed me to best him in matches. Not so much fun for him, and it resulted in his loss of interest in tennis. He then began to demand that I play with him on the basketball court where he could soon tire me out. That's what I get for playing tennis for myself and not for him, or for us both!

Competitive sports are not as imaginative or free or spontaneous as play created by children, or as any game that has no winners or losers. In our camps we have unorganized play time every day, in which all the adults stretch themselves, throw away competitiveness and embarrassment, and play whatever the children want to play. We try to make sure each child has at least one adult playmate to command, doing what and how the children wish them to do, and that the children are empowered to succeed and excel. This means a lot of crawling around with crawlers, peek-a-boo with infants, trampoline jumping, raft paddling, horsy rides and battles between sword-wielding knights astride middle-aged men, pillow fights, and that great favorite, a huge water fight ending with all adults soaked and dripping.

There are many new games that are fun, some area variations of hide and seek, tag, or musical chairs – you can invent your own. A favorite of our community was "Do you love me, Baby?" The person who is "it" must say only that to another person and try to elicit a laugh by the manner or expression of their saying it. The other must respond "I love you, Baby, but I just can't smile" with a serious face. If they break down and smile or laugh they become "it". I they can answer with a straight face the questioner gets two more chances to ask and try to get a laugh, after which they must try someone else.

Many happy cries, and of course sometimes tears. But that's a good thing, remember? The exertion, the bewilderment, the pure fun and laughter may well provide an occasion for tears that have been waiting for such a moment of tension or release to allow relief from buried distress. When it happens there are adults right there who understand, who kneel or sit with the child, put an arm around him, who tell him it's okay, to let it all out, that crying is a good thing. Only remember that whenever a child cries what he or she needs is for someone to be close and paying attention to what is needed, even if that may be only feeling safe and cared about. Maybe he or she will put a head on the adult's chest and just bawl. Eventually it will have been enough and away they go to play, all sparkles and aglow.

That reminds me of a story about a boy, around 8 years old, whom I liked a lot because of his liveliness and humor. But I felt bad for him because he was also troubled and fought a lot when his dark side came out. I watched his jaunty confidence crumble whenever he had to go home and knew he would be subjected to the harsh demeaning violent attitudes he was modeling with the other children. One day a smaller boy was crying, and all the other children, led by this boy, were taunting "Cry baby, Cry baby!" So I waded in, hugged the victim and told all the children he was doing just the right thing, that when people are hurt or sad they need to cry. I said I knew that all of them cried sometimes, but that was good, because if they don't cry enough when they are young, when they grow up they will have to pay a lot of money to psychiatrists.

The children all absorbed this information thoughtfully. I had well established that I was an ally and on their side, so they took whatever I offered, which often differed from all the other messages they got at home or in school. On another day I was shocked to find the smaller boy wailing as my rowdy little guy was pummeling him. I pulled him off and looked him in the eyes.

"What are you doing?" I demanded.

"Well," replied my rascal with a mischievous gleam, "you told us that crying was good for us – I was only helping the kid out!"

I joined all the children in a burst of laughter as I hugged both boys and said,

"I guess I forgot to tell you it doesn't help to hurt anyone. Since all of us get hurt, I suppose I thought you all understood that. Wrestling can be fun sometimes, but no hitting, because that hurts. What you need to learn is not to add to the hurting, but how to help each other. How to stop anyone from hurting anyone, and how to listen to anyone who is hurting."

I think, I hope they got my amended message too. I do know that many years later I would meet some of my students who had grown up and started their own families, and all of them told me I was the teacher they really listened to, that things I told them stayed with them and now help with their own children.

After the birth of our second son, Emmy and I made our home into an annex of the town day care center, and for a season we spent our days not only with our two boys but also with seven or eight children of working parents. It was, as you may imagine, an excellent and exhausting ground for us to try the practice of Parent Effectiveness Training and the teachings of Re-evaluation Counseling that we were just learning.

Those teachings reinforced our desire to respect children's feelings and went beyond other ways I had read about in not just understanding and allowing, but encouraging and being pleased with their expression. We saw how our patient attention gave them the safety to scream their anger and how quickly that tension was relieved and they became their fun-loving selves again. Without a lot of experience with children of that age, I just tried to stay close and be a resource when they looked for help. With Tashin not yet a year and Tokeem not yet four, and with a house full of energetic four and five year olds, we got a crash course in children's play and children's feelings. I saw that it didn't matter that I had no training and no theory. What mattered was that I was able to stay calm, be patient, listen and give real attention, and above all to show that I understood and cared. I also discovered that when I could be especially goofy it was the perfect medicine for almost every situation.

The next summer we bought an old school bus with our group. We were then meeting monthly to form a community which we called Mettanokit. In July of 1980 we all went to the International Rainbow Gathering being held that year in West Virginia. With our new community's help Emmy and I took over the childcare for the gathering.

In Arizona the previous summer I had, with my friend Joanne, known as Swami Mommy, helped to organize the child care for that large gathering. Childcare at the Rainbow Gatherings had been inaugurated in 1977 by my old friend, poet and clown, Wavy Gravy of the Hog Farm, which fed granola to 400,000 at the Woodstock Festival in 1969. Wavy also founded and directs Camp Winnarainbow for children with special needs. He called his Rainbow day care Kiddies City, but, being rather averse to urban life, I altered the name to Kid Village.

Our Mettanokit people, under Emmy's direction, taught the volunteers who came to help out our ways of giving patient and caring attention and joining in with the children's play when we saw they needed help. One of these volunteers felt so much in love with our new way of being with the children that she later bicycled all the way from her home to New Hampshire to join our community and help with our own children.

Another friend we made at that gathering was the delightful doctor clown Patch Adams, who came to teach with a comedy act about health and sanitation. We learned more – about the power and contagion of humor. Of course, the children all loved his presentation, and it was important for our community and for the work we continued to do at Rainbow Gathering Kid Villages from 1980 through 1989. Since then I have only found time to go to gatherings every five years or so, but Kid Village is still an important service there, and I hope this book may be a resource for them too.

The following spring our Mettanokit Community moved into its new home at Another Place, the conference center in New Hampshire where we had first come together three years before. Our first and most important order of business, as I have said, was to have a Re-evaluation Counseling teacher come over the mountain once a week to teach us all to co-counsel. A very wise move.

We all learned many important skills also from the conferences we hosted at Another Place, among them the New England Communities Conference, the New England Healing Arts Fair, and specialty conferences in Home Birth, Home Schooling, Permaculture, Organic Gardening, and particularly for us, the Re-evaluation Counseling Family Workshop.

The co-counseling family workshops that Patty Wipfler and Chuck Esser had devised are the basis of the play times that Ellika and I orchestrate today in our summer camps. The adults break into two groups, one making a circle to counsel with each other on the memories of their own childhoods, the other half going to play with the children.

The idea of the play is to put the children as much as possible in complete control, having them decide what and how they will play, and instructing the adults. With very small children and pre-verbal babies the adults are challenged to figure out games that allow the children to act powerfully. My sons are very good at this, and I have often watched Tashin, the younger one, as a sitting baby pushes him down howling with laughter each time as Tashin falls over helplessly again and again– for a half-hour or more! You can well imagine how much all little children love Tashin! Now he has his own daughter to play with – and is she powerful!

When the first group has completed their allotted play time, generally exhausted after wild chases, dueling with light sabers, jumping on the trampoline, playing horsy, or water fights, the group that was counseling takes their place and play continues while the first player group goes to counsel. They have much re-stimulation of old feelings to let out. No one ever played like that with us when we were that age!

Further detail about family work may be had from the address listed for Re-evaluation Counseling and the organization Hand-in-Hand Parenting (formerly Parents Leadership Institute, founded by Patty Wipfler – see Resources list in appendix).

> *"Your child may choose to do the kind of play you find most boring or most irritating, to see if you really will be delighted with her 'no matter what'... You may need to discharge in your own sessions about what you don't like about the play your child chooses, so that you can think about what the child is trying for and how to respond flexibly. When you can be enthusiastic about your child's choice of play ...trust will increase rapidly."*
> –Patty Wipfler, Hand in Hand Parenting founder

Are you hearing a voice in your head now that says, "This is all very well, but I don't have any time as it is. Where can I fit all this playing into my schedule?" If you are a single parent, or part of a nuclear pair that are both working, I really sympathize. But, you know, the young grow fast. Before you have time to think about it they're out of the house and raising their own families, and you are left with more memories of work than fun and joy in the children. That's the main reason I write this book. Parents need help. Our children should not have to find their way without an extended family and a community. We will think about that more in the last two chapters of this book.

Meanwhile you can get a lot of relief and a new understanding of this job of caring for children if you take the playful attitude as your basic mode. I know it's a stretch for you – it is for me, even though I am a pretty light-hearted individual who sees a lot of humor in life. My eleven-year-old grandson's energy is so high, and his taste in toys and games are so much not mine, that I have to push myself to enter in and be enthusiastic. But I try, especially recalling my toy soldiers and warplanes at his age, and we both benefit from that, as much and as long as I can manage it. Then I need a rest and a chance to let out my feelings with a fellow adult who can relate. In joining Linus to combat the Evil Empire I am able to engage him in thoughts and ideas and ask, in the role of his lieutenant, for his ideas and feelings about this engagement.

Be concerned, be understanding, but keep it light. In fact when we relax and get playful it is easier to be understanding and concerned, easier when we can insert some humor and fun into our responses.

I keep practicing this attitude – pulling myself out of my writer's habit of introspection to engage for a moment. I wave and make delighted or astonished expressions at children in the windows of passing cars. I poke my head into baby carriages on the street and give conspiratorial nods. I engage toddlers and babies in strollers in brief conversations. I sit and listen with amazement at the tales of four year olds. I always check in with the responsible adults and other grown-ups around – to assure them I am just being grandpa and not up to anything weird. Too bad that's part of our modern life, but we need to be conscious of it.

I love to go to playgrounds – usually it's with my grandson, so I have an apparent license to be there – then I can take time pushing other swings than his and helping tots onto the slides. If a child has a ball, I throw or kick it back and get an exchange going.

Ellika's house in Copenhagen is in a community of about twelve families known as Børneengen – the children's meadow. For three decades we have watched children be born to our families here and grow up free and safe, running in and out of everyone's houses, engaging us in play, sharing their perceptions of life. Many are now young adults and some have moved to their own houses. Børneengen has one dinner a week together, hosted by a different family.

The center of this community is a playground, the province of the day care center that extends along the western side. On the southeast edge Ellika's house fronts on the playground, and at our breakfast table we sit and watch the little ones pour in and chase each other in spontaneously made-up games all day. The young adult helpers, not so far from those ages, have a wonderful, relaxed knack for entering into their play when it seems needed or wanted, chasing and being chased, hugging and helping out. This continuous movie never stops until the end of day when parents reclaim their offspring.

This is a view I wish you all could have from your kitchen too. The chatter of children in their playhouse, the endless swinging of the swings, the rumble of the slides, the fantasies in the sand box, the races of the tricycles and skate boards, the screams of joy and the wails of sorrow, the explorations, the teamwork. When your heart is heavy, when you despair for the world, you need only peer from your window to have your faith and hope restored.

Another suggestion I would like to pass on from Larry Cohen. Empower girls and connect with boys. I don't have to explain that, do I? Our culture discourages the power and assertiveness of girls and discourages closeness and tenderness with boys. Pay attention to that. Challenge the girls to assert themselves, to do things for themselves, and praise them for that. If you are a man especially, wrestle with the boys and roll around with them (an acceptable male way of being physically close) but hug them too, especially when they cry, and let them know that is a wonderful thing to cry and you are really happy that they can do that.

So. Play.

Dr. Stuart Brown of The National Institute for Play suggests that people set aside 20 minutes a day to play with their children. Offer to play with your children and all children any time you can. It's a great honor when they let you into their world, the world of fun and creativity and "let's pretend." They love it when an adult wants to play with them and does it respectfully, considering their wishes and feelings. They want to show you and teach you. You will get closer. And it will be good for you too.

(See also the next chapter in this book about "Special Time" for more about how to make the most out of our time with children.)

The idea of parents playing with their children is a recent one in our present culture, but it is a good one, and important. Not just for the children, but for us all, for our relationships and for centering our lives more upon fun, about relaxing, easing stress, laughing, more about joy.

You can get many suggestions for ways to play in the recent book by Lawrence J. Cohen, PhD and Anthony T. Benedet, M.D.: *The Art of Roughhousing*. They mention that both monkeys and human children have a *play face* – a certain expression they adopt to signal to others that what they are doing is not *for real* but *play*. Roughhousing includes running, jumping, wrestling, falling, fighting – but an imitation of fighting, not serious. Roughhousing activates brain motor coordination, creativity, and enhances emotional attachment. They write, "When we stay calm and welcome our children's feelings we give them a safe and loving container for their emotions." Roughhousing, wrestling, play-fighting, fleeing and chasing games increase sharing, cooperation, and empathy as well as trust. It activates the sense of fairness, altruism, and the concept of win-win. We can be experts at play only by modeling extra enthusiasm, energy, and exuberance – the three "E"s. Not just before bedtime though – leave plenty of time to cool down, tune in and cuddle.

Playtime is important from the very beginning with a newborn all the way to – well, I'm eighty-five and play is still a big part of my life. I play with my grandchildren, and with young people at our camps and workshops, and I play tennis three times a week with old geezers like myself. I like not only keeping fit, but the fun and comradeship, sharing with a bunch of other old guys for a few hours every other day. I'm sure it keeps us going.

Next I want to tell you about one of the very best ways you can get closer to any child, build trust and understanding and lasting affection. In fact it could be a beautiful thing to share with any person, a friend, a partner, or a relative of your own.

Chapter Five
Special Time

"To get really close to a child you must find the time to be in his or her world together solely with him or her."

–Manitonquat

I placed that chapter on "play" very early in this book because it describes the most important attitudes and tools to bring to all the other subjects we will be talking about in caring for children. This chapter follows that up with a great gift we can give our children and ourselves, so that is why I have put it next. First absorb the principles of playing with young people, making them in charge feeling powerful and having fun. That is the secret of the extra magic of Special Time.

Special Time is indeed the most wonderful gift we can give to a child. Because we are giving our most precious possession – ourselves. And we are also giving the children themselves. So much of their experience of living in a world dominated by adults is shaped by our expectations and requirements about how they should behave. How they should be, actually. Their messages to us, in their language not ours, are little attended to by us, little considered or understood. And even Special Time we do too rarely, and usually not completely.

As I said in the last chapter, their world is the world of play. It is how they learn about the world they find themselves in, how they try to figure us adults into it, and express themselves to us. It is their language and their medium. If we want to understand them, then we must learn how they see themselves and the world around them by paying attention to their play. The more we play with them, on their terms, in their world, the more they become available to us, and the more we become available to them.

That is a wonderful way to become accessible – being fun for the child, nurturing continuing closeness and joy for the both of us. To get really close to a child you must find the time to be solely in that world together with her or him. No one else there, just the two of you playing in her world. No brothers or sisters or other children or adults to dilute the concentrated exploration together of the world as she shows it to you, of her thoughts and feelings about it. For this once, this Special Time, the child has you all to herself.

By your undivided attention she is assured how important she is to you, how important it is for you to learn her private thoughts and feelings. And the fun you experience together, the laughter and the joy are also personal to you both which you will treasure all your lives.

Special Time is an invitation you give to a child to spend a certain time together, only the two of you, in which you offer to do whatever the child wants to do. It is her time, and if it can happen often and on a regular basis it will be a time that the child will cherish and look forward to eagerly. After they have experienced how it will be, that they are in charge, that they can show their world and themselves, and that you will appreciate and be happy for that, that you are really there for them, eager to play and to learn of them, they will ask when they can have Special Time again.

What is important for you is that you are in such good shape that you can give your entire attention to them for the period of time you agree upon. In deciding how long the session will be, think about how long you will be able to give focused, thoughtful and interested attention to this child. If you are having a bad day and need attention yourself it's better to wait until your attention is really totally there for them. If it's at the end of a busy tough day for you, consider what it may take to un-stress yourself. So perhaps offer a time that might seem relaxed and pressure-free. Offer as much time as you think you can handle. If you think you have only attention enough for ten minutes, then that's what you give. Even if it's five minutes in the midst of everything, those five minutes can be very important, and much better than no attention at all, better than putting off the child's requests for attention all the time. Of course longer periods are better, when you are centered and can really be there for them. You have to determine that, and take care of yourself.

If it's only half an hour (maybe with a promise of more later) that's another solid step in building a deep connection between you. Consider setting aside a regular short period once a day. Think about the possibility of a whole morning, a whole afternoon, a whole evening, a whole day sometimes. Think about it. Imagine the wonderful explorations of his or her interests you could make – just the two of you, with him or her taking the lead and you happily following.

The main thing is to ensure that it stays truly the child's time. If any teaching is done, it is the child doing it – even if you know all about it already, you are so happy she wants to show off all she knows to you, so proud and grateful for her help. Be very careful about correcting any misinformation. Instead of contradicting, suggest perhaps it could be fun to research that area together with him taking the lead.

"When we make the time to fully concentrate on our relationships with our children, we satisfy some of the deep needs for loving and being close that are natural to people of every age."

–Patty Wipfler

Now that you know how to play with them, how to let them lead and be in charge of their world with you, you know the basic tool for Special Time. And the more you employ it the better you will get at it, the more you will enjoy it.

You might, as I did, consider taking a child on a longer trip with you and allocate some of the time on the journey just for Special Time together. I took my older boy on many long trips, to British Columbia, to Alaska, to Europe and other shorter ones. It was good for both of us. Not always easy when you need to give attention to your business, because you want to be able to find something he can safely enjoy without you for that period. But you have all the rest of that time together, riding in a car or a train or a plane, time to listen to him, time to explore interesting places. I took him to an International Indian Treaty Conference at White Earth Reservation in Minnesota, and to a Rainbow Gathering in Washington State where at 5 years old he helped me to prepare the child care area. I let him lead me everywhere in the gathering and explain to me what everyone was doing. We went also to a gathering on the Okanagan Reserve where he was introduced, at 7 years old, as my assistant. Which he surely was. I invited him to tell all the people what he could always say to keep me together with my spirits high, and with no hesitation he took the microphone and said "I love you, Daddy."

When I spoke at a peace conference in Anchorage I took Tokeem. Happily my brother lived in Kodiak then and was delighted to take his nephew for long periods while I was engaged in the conference. Tokeem had his first experience catching fish with a hand net on a pole in Cook Sound. He also got to meet my co-speaker, astronaut Edgar Mitchell, who had walked on the moon. When he was thirteen I took him on one of my tours in Europe.

In all these trips we were alone most of the time. I answered questions – he was and is ever curious and an avid learner. But he spent even more time exploring on his own and then telling me about his discoveries.

His mother, Emmy, had a regular weekly Special Time date with him, and at a certain stage he always wanted to go to the shopping center and play games on the machines in the arcade. He mostly enjoyed teaching her how to play each of the games.

She wrote an article later telling the story of a particular Special Time when she had decided not to speak all day in remembrance of a friend who had died. She asked Tokeem if he would like to change to another day, but he said no, he would still like his Special Time with her at the arcade. As they drove the half hour journey Tokeem talked. He talked more than he would normally do if she were responding. When they got there he was so full of things to say that they never went into the arcade but spent the whole time walking up and down the mall while he talked and she listened. He kept talking in the car on the way home, and when they got back she turned off the engine and sat there while he talked for quite a while more!

Now you must understand that Emmy's profession is family

counselor, an excellent one, and she spends a lot of her time listening to children and getting them to open their thoughts and feelings to her. She was astonished that after all those years Tokeem could spend all that time pouring out heart, mind and soul as he never had before. All she had to do was shut up!

Another time Tokeem and I went camping on October Mountain in the Berkshires. I had gotten two free tickets to a weekend of classical concerts by the Boston Symphony at Tanglewood. He was the only one in our community interested to come with me. He asked what it would be like, I gave him an idea of what to expect, that we could camp at night and in the day picnic on the grass and listen to the sounds from the music shed. He asked if he could take comic books and we loaded him up with enough of those. We pitched a tent and built a fire, and he told me the story lines of many of his comic books. During the concerts he asked questions about what was being played, and then read his books as we listened. At the last concert Sunday afternoon I offered the information that the soloist playing had done more to bring the interest of the public to his instrument than anyone in that century. Tokeem got up and strode into the shed, all the way down the aisle, and stood below the soloist for a long time, then returned. He asked me the soloist's name and repeated it when I told him.

No more was said then, but when we got home the community was all eager to hear how he liked the concerts. He smiled and told them proudly:

"I heard Jean-Pierre Rampal!"

Of course I now wish I had taken more advantage of those wonderful years of their growing and had offered more Special Time to my boys – and to the other children in our community. I was only beginning then to learn all the things I am sharing with you now. The years fly by so fast, and we don't realize until they are past – as in Malvinas Reynolds's song – "Turn around and he's two, turn around and he's four, turn around and he's a young man going out of your door."

I can remember watching Tashin sleeping on my bed when he was about nine and thinking, "he won't stay like this, before I know it he'll be gone." Now they have both started their own families and I am looking forward to Special Time with my grandchildren.

I remember some Special Times with Tashin – the time he asked me to make a bow and arrows for him, and I was so terrible at it, but he enjoyed it all anyway. The walks we used to take in the woods, checking on the wild turkeys, the hole where the fox kept her kits, the beaver pond and the otters playing. It wasn't until he was a teenager that we had some of our best times. As an old sailor I had asked Tokeem if he wanted to go sailing, but he said no, sailing did not interest him, but I should ask Tashin because he liked it. So Tashin and I began sailing and had many good times together, exploring the streams and marshes of the Merrimac River delta. Once a storm came up and we hauled the little boat on the shore and huddled under its shelter upside down. But best of all were the longer times when I would rent a cabin sloop, and we would explore Cape Anne and Cape Cod and Massachusetts Bay, taking food and a camp stove and sleeping bags. Just the two of us at sea, me mostly listening and answering questions – we really got close during those times.

In August of 1995 we were at berth in Gloucester, and I recalled I was on a similar cruise at his age, 15, with my father in 1945, and how we were at a restaurant when a howl came from the street and a mob of people burst in to shout that the war was over, Japan had surrendered! It was one of the very few good times I could remember with my own father, whom I did not see very much growing up. And there I was fifty years later with my son, watching the fireworks.

I have always held those memories among the greatest treasures of my life. I was so glad to hear a grown-up Tashin tell our friends when we traveled to a gathering in Brazil in 2003 that those were also some of his best memories.

Like most men, when I look back I regret my lost chances and that I had not spent more Special Time with my boys individually. I often wish we had gone fishing more, or camping, or canoeing. What

I managed to do was so good for me. Was it that good for them? All I can tell you is that today in their thirties they are much better fathers than I was. The way they are with *all* children is a perfect example and model for us all of how to be with young people. They are endlessly patient, listening, paying attention to and understanding the children's perspectives and feelings. They are considerate, giving choices but holding firmly to necessary limits, not getting angry, staying mostly light, funny, playing, wrestling, and hugging a lot. If all children had such fathers we would surely have arrived in Paradise!

Family vacations, camping trips and so on, are good chances for the family to get closer. They are not Special Time, which is one adult with one child, full attention on the child and doing what the child wants to do. But Special Times can be arranged within the trip, each adult inviting each child at different times to do something the child suggests. These times provide a change, variety for everyone and bring everyone closer.

Special Time should be an uninterrupted time – no business, no cooking, no cleaning, no telephone, no doorbell, no other children or people demanding your attention. A relaxed time, when you are rested and ready to devote yourself to being totally present, noticing everything about the child, hearing all she says, but also her tones of voice, movements, postures, facial expressions. The child is brand new in this moment – take her all in and learn her.

You have invited her to make this her time – at first she may not know what to do with this reversal of roles, but as you are eager to do whatever she wants she will begin to try you out. If she feels your enthusiasm for her suggestions, by your really enjoying doing what she wants, she will start to explore the possibilities and figure out for herself how she can use your attention. She will begin to show more of herself to you, show feelings and express thoughts that in the busy flow of ordinary life with others around she has had no opportunity to show. Your love and interest in her make it feel safe for her.

You may feel tempted to "help" her play, to show better ways, to guide or teach. Resist the temptation. If you do try to direct, you will miss learning about her feelings, her preferences, her ideas, what makes her laugh, what really annoys her, what is fun and joyful for her.

Even if you are finding her activity dull or boring or far from your own taste, it will be much better if you show interest and all the enthusiasm you can muster. That will pay off in getting you closer. Now when she wants to play with make-up is not the time to mention the oppressive indoctrination of the young by cosmetic companies – keep that conversation for another time, and rehearse how to present it then in a way that does not detract from her enjoyment and creativity at the make-up table.

Children are always learning (and learn best when we are not trying to teach), and they will use your attention to explore and test the frontiers of their experience. Will you support their explorations? How much mess can they make? How dirty can they get? How much noise can you stand? No doubt you will have limits, and they want to know them. It makes the world safer for them. But it's best if the limits we impose are only ones for their health and safety, not for our convenience. It's okay if we have to put extra clothes in the wash and take time to clean up messes – the fun and the learning that gave us that work was really worth it. If they are given a limit they will probably object. They will want to know why, and they should be told in a way they can understand – ("because I said so" is not a reason). If they are upset they need to be listened to and understood – they will not be ready to hear your rationale while they are upset. "You are upset," you say, "You really wanted to do that. I'm sorry, but you may not." You just stay calm and patient and loving and ride out the upset but holding the limit. Later you can refer back to it and explain more about why and perhaps suggest other choices. More about setting limits in a later chapter.

If Special Time is a regular and expected event you will notice changes in the child and in your relationship. Feelings of closeness and intimacy, of a new and deeper relationship will grow as well – a natural and frequent showing of affection, a general enjoyment of being together any time, and an eagerness in anticipation of Special Time with you. You will be made more aware of the difficulties she has as they come up, what is causing her trouble with school, teachers, friends, siblings, and because of the trust that has been created she will come more often to you for advice and help.

"Decide to notice everything about your child's words, expression, tone of voice, posture, and movement. Absorb information through your every pore, as if your child were entirely new to you! Let her know you are enjoying her thoroughly. Let your affection, interest, and approval show on your face, in your voice, and through your touch."

–Patty Wipfler

When you bring the skills discussed in the last chapter that you have been practicing in your play with children, you will be able to learn much more about this young person. By taking on the weaker (smaller, stupider, clumsier, more helpless) role and giving her the stronger (bigger, smarter, more competent, and powerful) role she may show in play many places that are difficult for her. You may be asked to play the part of the baby, or the little sister, or the pupil, while she takes the opportunity to turn the tables playing the mama, the big sister, the teacher. This occasions great fun for her. Play the comic part of the clueless, bumbling fool she has to correct. Pay attention to her laughter, and where it happens – really go for that, ham it up, use funny voices and dumb facial expressions, do pratfalls and have fun being the comedy fool. (Those have to be modified for teenagers – take your cues from them – if they laugh you are on track.) Cry in terror from his or her threats and run for your life. If the game is for you to chase her, then you almost catch her but are unable to hold her and let her get away again and again. Check over the last chapter on play again. The child's laughter shows what she is working on.

It's fun to be a fool. I know. Early in my career I was one professionally. As a teenager I had learned the great power of getting laughs from an audience of my peers. We all laughed at the things that were hard for us, that were oppressive and hurtful and stupid and confusing – it was how we assured ourselves we were okay and superior to anything that wanted to hurt us. The explosions of laughter I got as a teenage comedian on stage were like ambrosia and nectar – they fed my soul. And made me feel part of a teen conspiracy. In my early twenties I was part of a very successful comedy act – my friend Dick Brown being the wit to my lovable dumb fool. We had a great year before enthusiastic audiences until he became engaged to a respectable young woman who made it clear she did not intend to be a show-biz wife, so I went back to the university to study theater.

Your parents and colleagues may wonder about you becoming the village idiot, but don't let that stop you. Dump your dignity and see what fun it can be. Tell them you don't want Daffy Duck to get all the laughs at home. But, please, stay away from sarcasm – too many of us adults are tempted to use that on children – it's not funny. Sarcasm is criticism and a way of being superior – and that will not get you closer. Let me say that again:

**Sarcasm is criticism – a way of being superior
– it will not get you closer.**

Of course it's not only laughter that may come up when the emotions of play are riding high. When anxiety, tears, or anger emerge you must be ready and present in your role of compassionate listener. Encourage a full discharge of those feelings, staying present as a steady base of love and understanding. If you can hear all the child's feelings without trying to change, direct or divert them, she will express them fully and return to her playful nature with renewed confidence.

The one thing that I hear most often from old characters of advanced years like myself is that, looking back on our times as parents of young children, we never realized how brief that period would be. We all regret not having spent more not just "quality" time but quantity time with our children. Special Time is the highest quality time, because it is distilled and concentrated with each child alone. Time to relax and step out of other roles to be with a child is not easy to come by, but it is so precious it ought to be a top priority. It builds close relationships and strengthens the bond between you and that very special young person, a bond that becomes more import to you both as you grow older.

If you are a parent you worry that you may not be doing a good enough job at it – I am pretty sure you are, comes with the territory, your reading this book is evidence of it –you can gain confidence by playing and especially playing while sharing Special Time as often as you can. Gives you more chances to show your love. And what can you do for yourself that is more important? What can you do for a child that will be more important, more welcome and appreciated? It's good for you both. Good for the whole family, the community, the world.

Chapter Six
The Art of Listening

"Individual thinking is greatly enhanced by attentive, non-responsive listening."

—Harvey Jackins

Now I would like to explain the theory of discharge that has been part of these discussions. For more than sixty years this theory has been being developed by many people, building trust and closeness, building community. We have kept current with those explorations and experiences through community circles, newsletters, workshops, conferences, journals, books, and audio and video recordings as the process has continued to develop.

All of that has been central to my own parenting and teaching, so I will attempt a very brief sketch of what I take to be the main ideas that might help you understand why they work so well in practice and guide you in approaching interactions with children and with all people.

In Chapter One I described what I see in all newborn babies that indicates the basic qualities of inherent human nature, built into by our genes by biology and evolution. This gives us a basis for looking at who we are. We notice that we are innocent, curious, playful, fun-loving, creative and caring beings who love to get close and touch and tell stories and listen and laugh and do things, to make things, to dance, sing, and – somehow – to be helpful, to make life better for others as well as for ourselves.

We do like to cooperate and do things together. We like exercising our bodies and our minds, and we like to experience love and beauty and joy. We are interested in animals and like to make friends with them, we like plants, flowers, trees, fruits, and we like food. All positive things. We do not like to be hurt and, as we learn the connection, we do not like to hurt others. We naturally feel compassion for those we love and even for strangers, and that grows as we learn and grow in the world.

All I have learned in a long lifetime of watching children at home, in nurseries, day-care and playgrounds, and listening to people's stories in private sessions, in groups, in prisons, through counseling colleagues, through journals and other literature, including social and psychological research, has served to confirm these observations.

So if this positive model of our original nature is valid, how come we have all these problems with ourselves and with each other? As you could expect, the answer is complex and no doubt incomplete, but the explanation we are figuring out so far helps very well in our practice, and since, for me, effectiveness is the best measure of truth, it is good enough.

It seems that our human constitution is quite adaptable and has automatic systems of healing. When our skin is lacerated or our bones broken, they will knit – of course it helps if we bind them together while that happens. When we get infections our bodies work to expel them through discharge – through coughing, sneezing, emitting pus or mucus, sweating, vomiting, excreting, and so on.

Likewise when our emotions are assaulted and traumatized we have a natural discharge process that facilitates their healing. Babies exhibit this very early. When they cry it is not only and always because they are hungry or physically uncomfortable. We cannot ask and may not know what is wrong, but if we hold them while they cry, if we speak soothingly and regard them with concern and affection, they will cry it out and then completely relax, usually fall sound asleep, and be alert and happy when they wake.

Emotional hurts have a social component, they involve people. Other people have a definite part in this process, analogous perhaps to the binding of physical wounds. Fear, sadness, anger and other upsets usually have a cause that involves a person or persons doing or not doing something. Of course we can be frightened by a natural threat like thunder, or sad at our loss of something dear to us, or frustrated by a machine, but even then it is human comfort and understanding that best helps us to recover.

So when a baby or child is hurt and cries, perhaps screams or shakes, if she has a safe and caring person that she trusts holding her, giving her attention and assurance that he will be available, the child will discharge her feelings until they subside. If no one is there to give that attention and assurance, or if whoever may be there ignores the cry or reacts negatively to it, she may stop her discharge before it is complete and the hurt is recorded in her memory. For children who are abandoned or abused these memories of emotional hurt can accumulate to the extent of requiring therapy or if unattended may create sociopathic or psychopathic conditions.

Most people, while they may not experience such extreme mistreatment, carry a certain amount of unhealed distress but manage to press on and somehow organize and maintain their lives at a tolerable level. We may complain – it's not ideal – but we can live with it. For people who can afford psychotherapy there may be opportunities to improve their lives. But for that help it is not necessary to find an expert who exacts high fees to pay for his years of schooling and his expensive lifestyle. All that is really needed is someone with whom you feel safe, whom you trust, who will trade a session of her attention and natural helpful compassion for a session of your giving the same to her.

The medicine is love, of course. Caring, compassion, well-wishing, whatever you call it, it is natural to us all. We really do want to help others, although our conditioning makes it difficult, almost impossible to ask others for help. But once we agree we want and need to help each other all we need to learn is how to listen. To listen in a way that allows them, encourages them, to discharge the old emotions that keep pushing their way to the surface causing distress and confusion, and getting in the way of clear thinking and decisive acting.

What we need to learn is the art of listening. Listening to enable the other to locate and discharge those old distress recordings. In this art there are two general types of listening. We might call them passive and active, or permissive and non-permissive.

Passive, or permissive listening can be very powerful. When you are learning this art you have the chance to be only attentive and sympathetic and you don't have to worry about saying or doing the wrong thing. You will see quite marked results of your attention. If you are listening to someone also new to this process, you can be sure that, like everyone, she has not often had the opportunity of such uninterrupted attention. Most people are too busy or too preoccupied with their own distress and their own stories to want to listen to us for long without interrupting. So when we find someone who really wants to hear our stories and can empathizes with our feelings, it all pours out. The effectiveness of the therapy of passive listening depends only on it's depth and intensity, and with that discharge noticeable, often remarkable transformations occur.

Active, or non-permissive listening can be very useful when the person who is being listened to cannot remember or loses the thread of memories. Blank. No thoughts or feelings. Confused, lost or numb. Speaking only superficially, not knowing what to say.

Whether you are being an active or a passive listener, it is best to be thinking carefully about what the other is saying. Trying to relate to the feelings of the other while being only passive it is of course still good to react to what is being said with a nod or a shake of the head, a squeeze of the hand, a sigh or a giggle while empathizing with the other that does not interfere with the discharge. If she is confused about her feelings or is not aware of feelings at all you can become active in helping her discover and express those feelings. That discharge is what you are both seeking. It is the agent of the insight and new thinking that will produce re-evaluation, greater awareness, and change. Change happens with insight and understanding of the causes of the feelings, and with a decision about ways to contradict those feelings and then deciding on and taking a new action to do so.

Your help may come in the form of questions that may lead to memories and feelings that are buried below consciousness, or statements about her life and her character that help to contradict the assaults and the distress imbedded by them that block the full power of her intelligence, her creativity, her caring and her aliveness and vitality, her joy and excitement in life.

With thought and practice and further understanding of the person you can learn better and better what will help her to discharge. Discharge has a number of different manifestations.

First there is the discharge of just speaking about one's life. We don't get many opportunities to do that to supportive listeners, and just the narration of our experiences gets a lot off our chest, so to speak. Tears are a discharge that may come from sadness – or sometimes from happiness or relief, sometimes from a display of love, compassion, caring or generosity that contradicts the inhuman apathy that surrounds us.

Laughter is a discharge of course, that may proceed from the comedic undoing of arrogance, pomposity, aggressive stupidity and so on, but often also from fear. Releasing small fears or embarrassment. Bigger fears generally provoke cold sweat, shaking, sometimes goose-flesh, but sometimes also laughter, as I have known people who avoid funerals because they produce in them inappropriate uncontrollable laughter.

Yawning is also a discharge – usually of physical tension. As a young man in speech class I learned to provoke yawns to relax my larynx for a deep resonant vocal tone. When I was performing professionally there would always be, at the most nervous moments just before the rise of the curtain on a large expectant audience, a whole line of actors and singers practicing their yawn backstage for relaxation. People experienced in using discharge will often yawn to relieve tension and perhaps open avenues of feeling and memory that could provoke deeper discharge.

So when the one you listen to yawns, or giggles, when you notice the eyes begin to water or the hand you hold begin to sweat, you may be certain something is happening inside, something is beginning to shift.

You can apply this knowledge to understand the spontaneous discharge that sometimes occurs unexpectedly in ourselves and others, in babies and older children, in sudden outbursts of tears of laughter or anger, trembling, yawning, or gooseflesh. If there is no reasonable cause apparent for these we can understand that some recording below our awareness is being re-activated. From an infant to an elder, when anyone is discharging it is best not to interfere, not to distract or engage in dialogue, but only to attend compassionately and allow the discharge to run its natural course. A healing is going on at that time. Laugh or cry or shake your head in sympathy as you listen, but not so much as to draw attention to yourself. Afterwards it is helpful to listen to the person's thinking about the feelings and memories that may have been stirred, and any new thoughts or decisions that might arise from them.

It is important, in terms of our caring for children, to understand that they are not equipped and should not be obliged to deal with our negative feelings, and that we can use this discharge process to clear these feelings in order not to confront our children with them. Do not, therefore, use a child as your counselor. The negative feelings that are distressing you in the present are powered by patterns derived from old experiences going back to your childhood, and they can best be handled by discharging those earlier feelings with an adult listener. For this it is best to have a regular listener friend who knows your story and can understand and support you well. With your listener's encouragement you can consign those feelings to the past and make good, clear and calm choices with the child in the present. If, for instance, a child has done something or is behaving in a way that upsets you, connect with your friend to discharge before you try to connect with the child. And if there is no time you might try a brief telephone session: "Can you give me five minutes? I'm about to lose it here! Yowwwhhh!"

If no one is available, go for a walk or scream into your pillow, or take a bunch of calming deep breaths – five seconds in, five seconds out. Remind yourself then that the best way to deal with any situation with a child is to connect, calmly and with unconditional love and caring – listen and hug.

In a pinch it is also possible to make a stranger into a supportive listener. I was alone in a small Pennsylvania town after visiting a native circle in a federal prison there. The only thing of interest in town was a movie theater that was showing *Platoon*, which I had heard was very good so I went in to see it. It was more than good, it was realistic and an excruciating emotional experience that left me shattered. I staggered from the theater shaken and stunned and went into the small town park. One woman sat alone at a bench.

"Could I speak to you a few minutes?" I asked, "I have just seen a very upsetting film and I need to talk to someone about the feelings it gave me."

She nodded, a bit tentatively, and I sat down and began to tell about the picture. Soon I was sobbing and weeping, and she reached over and took my hand and just held it comfortingly until I had let it out and could think and discuss my feelings and thoughts about war in general and the Vietnam War in particular. I thanked her for listening and she thanked me for sharing my feelings and my thoughts as well with her, and I listened as she shared feelings that she said she had never shared with anyone.

I went back to my hotel feeling enriched by just a half hour of true closeness with another human soul whom I would never see again but will never forget.

When you observe friends or strangers in distress you can become a supportive listener and be of wonderful help to them. One day when we were walking in a small city park Emmy and I observed a harried woman screaming with rage at her toddler, dragging her roughly by one arm and punctuating their progress with occasional mighty swats on the child's diapered bottom, lifting her a bit off the ground each time.

All over the park people stopped to watch, probably wondering what their responsibility was – should they interfere? As I expected Emmy went into action immediately and headed to intercept the woman on the path ahead.

The mother paused in her anger at the child to glare at the people watching, a look challenging anyone thinking of interfering. Seeing Emmy bearing down on her and me right behind her defenses began to bristle, preparing a rebuff like, "This is my child, don't you dare…"

This was to be an informative encounter, I knew, and I stayed outside but close enough to take in what would be the response. Before the woman could say anything Emmy smiled at her.

"It's hard being a mother sometimes, isn't it?"

"Tell me about it! The mother said wearily, obviously relieved for a non-judgmental human connection.

"Why don't we sit down on the bench here and you can tell me about it?" Emmy responded.

So they did. Emmy listened sympathetically to the woman's flood of woes, maternal, marital and social – the struggle of trying to do everything for everybody with no help, no support, and no appreciation.

By the time the mother had discharged all the pressures that had been suppressed in her, her demeanor had utterly changed. She spoke with Emmy as with an old friend, and even laughed as Emmy lightly offered a few tips for handling her distress and her child and validated the mother's love and hope and her value and importance in the lives of her child and family.

With babies, just to show we are pleased with them, hugging and playing with them, and imparting the sense that all is well, will help them to live in the present moment and view it with trust and contentment.

When a child has feelings but is not discharging them you can help by asking them to tell what happened to a sympathetic audience – even of strangers. I was in a park one day giving a talk, and a woman approached me later with a little girl by the hand. She said her daughter had been stung by a bee, that she was not allergic, but seemed to be very subdued now, not herself. I could see the child was very shut down, not like a normal unrepressed four-year-old. There was no light in her, she was somehow lost and hiding.

I made a quick guess that she had not discharged about the pain and fear sufficiently, and I also thought the mother, who seemed very concerned, had tried to offer her comfort, but that the child probably had shut herself down in order not to distress her mother. It often happens that without trying to distract or divert a child's distress, the child picks up on the mother's worry and pretends everything is all right so as not to cause her upset.

I got down on my knees to be at her level and said, in an interested and calmly concerned tone,

"So – you were stung by a bee!"

The child instantly burst into tears and showed me the mark of the sting on her arm, but quickly got control again and shut herself down to her former blank and passive face. I told the mother to take the child to each of the groups of picnickers about the meadow and ask her to tell them the story about the bee.

About an hour later the mother came back, alone, to tell me what had happened. She said at first the child repeated the story with many tears, showing off the swelling of the sting. After several times the story got shorter and shorter, the quick and matter-of-fact in a bored monotone, and then finally she ran away to play with other children with all her joy and sparkle returned.

That story can also remind us that even when we may think we have discharged enough of an incident or a feeling, there very well may be more if we go back and keep going back until we can really feel it is just old stuff and not with us any more now.

Recent research is indicating that even tiny pre-verbal infants pick up our distresses by our tones, and that measurable changes in their brains happen as they do. It's not safe to express our negative feelings near a sleeping baby either, because they have also measured those brain changes taking place as distressful sounds of anger and hurt are transmitted to them through headphones.

Well, none of us are perfect yet, all we can do is keep learning and trying to make it better for our children as we do. They understand we are not perfect, and if we stay connected, keep listening and caring, they will forgive anything. You have always done the best you knew, and it will keep getting better. I know. Because here you are!

So – one more story to illustrate that.

One day when my oldest boy was nine I came into the room the boys shared to find them fighting. They had their squabbles and we generally let them work it out between them, but this had gotten very physical and Tokeem was angrily wailing on Tashin who was not yet six, trying to ward off blows and getting the worst of it. My sense of fair play was outraged, but worse was the thought that my beloved firstborn had become a bully. So, bursting with undischarged feelings about bullies in my own childhood, I leapt into the fray without thinking, grabbed Tokeem by his shoulders and shook him firmly to emphasize my upset.

"What are you doing, Tokeem?" I demanded.

Shocked at my unheard of action (we never touched any child in anger) he only stared to adjust himself to this behavior from me, and then sternly pointed at the door.

"Out!" he demanded, "out of my room!"

That brought me quickly to my senses, and I realized the enormity of what I had done, nodded dumbly, and with my tail between my legs like a chastised puppy, I left.

It was enough to change the tenor of the fight. Whatever it was about it was over. I spent the next hour wandering in shame and confusion about the main house of our community. I felt I had broken the strong bond between me and Tokeem, and I wondered if and how it could ever be repaired. How could I do such a thing? I was completely disconsolate.

Thinking about it, I realized that of course, of the two of them, it was Tokeem who needed my listening, my understanding and appreciation of his feelings. I should have remembered from my work in the prisons that the perpetrator is also a victim. I should have understood that Tokeem was hurting and needed my understanding, not my outrage and anger.

When I got back to our huge kitchen I saw him sitting at the other end talking to another adult member. I considered ruefully how I might apologize and explain, but then he looked up and saw me. Without hesitation he jumped up and ran across the room and threw his arms around me, and we embraced and wept together.

A bond so deeply formed from birth is not easily damaged. He knew me well enough that he could understand my upset and forgive my unthinking response. It was the only time in our lives that my touch was anything but loving and thoughtful. When you are that connected your children will understand and forgive your mistakes.

Especially when you apologize.

Part Three

"What actually spoils a child…punishment, separation, and rejection."

–Jan Hunt

Chapter Seven
Punishment

"The child is always innocent."

—Alice Miller

Never punish a child.
Never. Ever. Period.

Chapter Eight
Can't You Control That Child?

"In changing a person's opinions, listening is a more effective tool than talking."

–Harvey Jackins

So, I made the last chapter short and simple, for emphasis, to get your attention, to help you remember. Now I can tell you why.

First – what are your needs, your goals and wishes for children in your care? Probably you want them to behave well, to be cooperative, helpful and kind to others. You also want them to be able to take care of themselves, to be safe and healthy, and you would like them to have an active curiosity, an alert, engaged mind that likes to learn and so learns well. What else do you require of them?

Now think about that. Seriously, do you think it will help them achieve all that if you make them feel worse? Do you think they will listen to you better and have more respect for you if you punish them, hurt them physically or emotionally or take away freedoms and privileges?

Children are not bad. If they act in a hurtful way it is because they have experienced a hurt that has not been discharged fully and understood and they have not been helped to recover their natural disposition of helpfulness, caring, playfulness, and curiosity.

Adding a hurt to a hurt is not helpful.

This applies also to our criminal justice system.

The people in our prisons were once innocent children who got hurt and kept getting hurt more without ever being heard and understood and helped. Every prisoner in the circles my wife and I lead wants to be good, wants to be helpful, wants to make a positive contribution somehow. No matter what terrible thing they have done it was not the choice of the young person they once were. Most of them can still be helped to heal from the hurts they have experienced, and they would like to help others do the same, help young people from being hurt as they were.

But that's for another book.

I can tell you out of eight decades of personal experience as child and man, father and teacher and counselor, that punishment doesn't work. And all the research supports that conclusion, that it does not prevent or deter bad behavior in the long run, not in family, not in education, not in business, and not in our criminal justice system.

"Punishment, criticism, blame or reproach…is never called for, never justified, and never effective."
—Harvey Jackins

When children are uniformly treated well and helped to have a better understanding of themselves, when they are helped to have a higher self-esteem, they are less defiant, less antagonistic, they don't join in bullying of weaker children but are more likely to interrupt mistreatment. Relations with siblings are closer and more caring. Those children tend to be more hopeful and optimistic, tend to be peacemakers, fixers, healers not hurters.

I hear people say, "Nothing wrong with punishment – spare the rod and spoil the child. Look at me, I turned out all right. You didn't mess with my dad, he'd lay a hurt on you with his belt. But I'm better for it today." And I think to myself, "*are* you?" I know this guy has plenty of problems with himself, as well as with his children and his employees, that he would not have if he had had a close and affectionate relationship with his father.

I remember a men's circle we had on a mountain camping trip some thirty years ago. Twenty of us sat around a fire under a full moon, and one man after the other began to talk about his father. There was not one good father-son relationship in that whole circle. The fathers were either absent, or they were indifferent, or harshly dominating and punitive. That experience has been confirmed and repeated through my many years of counseling men about their childhoods. With that image of fatherhood I felt lucky to have an absent father who didn't care to have any paternal connection with me.

When it comes to corporal punishment there should by now be no doubt – but although it is banned in many civilized countries, spanking is still legal in the US. A research study of 36,000 individuals indicates that non-abusive corporal punishment has an adverse effect on children and not the desired lesson in morality or following the rules laid down for them. It showed that children receiving such punishment had not lesser but greater delinquent and aggressive behavior, that they had more mental health problems and worse relationships with their parents. This form of punishment was shown much more to likely to grow into abuse of children. There was often a short-term compliance but none in the long-term. Later in life those so punished were more likely to manifest anger in aggression and violence. They were more prone to anxiety, clinical depression, addition to drugs, abuse of their spouses, and criminal behavior. Today most organizations recommend trying alternative forms of punishment without physical hurt.

We can look at some of those alternatives that are suggested these days in a moment, but I want you to consider the idea that punishment of any kind puts up a barrier. It tells the child that he or she is unacceptable, bad in some way, stupid or lazy or just trying to create problems. No one wants to think that of himself, so the child will begin to defend and most likely to hide, to lie and do whatever else an intelligent person might do to protect against a more powerful enemy force. The important thing then is to stay on the child's side, to be an ally and not an enemy. We need to preserve closeness and trust, to be able to discuss the issue, listening empathetically to the child. Children do have a strong sense of fairness and justice, and any decision that is arrived at with the participation and agreement of the child is more likely to be observed. A very helpful tool is to offer the child a choice of alternative actions that would be acceptable.

Probably many of you were punished in various ways – perhaps not beaten, but made to feel badly – and you are doing all right while your friends and parents may be telling you that you need to be more strict, that you need to control that wild child.

I know my young single mom felt the weight of pressure from her family and the culture. She felt that because she had no man she had to be not only the nurturing, encouraging, tender mother she naturally was, but once she had to force herself, as she said, to do "the man's job" of punishing me when I misbehaved. I can remember her whipping me that once, with a thin willow branch on my bare legs while I danced and screamed. I could not believe that my safe and reliable and loving mother would do such a thing. It turned my world upside down. Scary.

But somehow I also felt her fear about me, and her confusion. And I felt the reality of her love for me, her only child, confirmed every day. So here was something about the world I just could not comprehend, and I could only accept it and keep my confusion to myself. There were some places in this world where I would find no help and would have to fend for myself.

I hope you understand that, crazy as it was, your punishing parents probably really did love you. Only sometimes they did not know how to show or express it. They were doing what they knew, and you figured out how to survive it, to take care of yourself and make a good life. If you had not, you would not be interested in reading this book.

Your parents did the best they could. They used what they had been taught, and perhaps they also learned to treat you a bit better than their parents had treated them. Perhaps they tried to be a little closer to you than their parents were to them. I hope so.

There are many ways to raise and to relate to children, and if a child can feel loved at all and have a safe home, they will get by. But the human psyche is fragile and can be more easily damaged than most people realize.

"Children lost in distress act it out and then get blamed."
–Tim Jackins

I want to tell you about one of the prisoners in one of my prison circles who had a background and a childhood quite different from most of the others. This prisoner was not from a broken home, like many, nor from a poor family, like most. His parents were quite wealthy, and he never wanted for any material thing. They were not at all strict with him, and they let him go his own way. With his money he could pretty much do and get whatever he wished.

So what's my point? If he was not punished, why did he go wrong? The point is he really was punished. Not intentionally, but he was neglected. He did not receive what every human being needs, requires to be whole, to feel good about himself, about life. He did not receive love.

Well, perhaps they did love him, or thought they did – in this culture we tend to think that material gifts are an indication of our love. Perhaps they thought that giving him complete freedom was also an expression of their love. I am sure you know that idea is false. What he was actually was abandoned.

Children need to be cuddled and held, they need to be close and know the people around them, be known themselves and appreciated for who they are. They want to feel they are wanted, that they belong. They want to do interesting and fun things with the family. Poor little rich boy, he was not loved, he was neglected, abandoned to find his way in a world of other neglected, abandoned, often abused young men, a world with easy access to drugs – a love substitute that can be bought.

There are many ways to punish.

Yes, there are many ways to punish and damage the tender young human psyche.

The reason most of us resort to punishment is fear. We are afraid for the health and safety of children who are in our care. We are afraid they will hurt themselves or hurt others, damage property, injure animals. We are afraid of other people's opinions, that they will judge or even openly criticize us in our treatment of children. We are even afraid of showing too much physical affection, innocent as it may be, lest our motives be suspect.

All that is mainly because we are so isolated in our relations with children (and because there are real dangers to children from predators damaged by that isolation). We have no support, as parents, as teachers, or in any other role of interacting with and caring for young people. That isolation will be treated in the considerations of the final two chapters of this book.

We punish out of fear. We punish out of anger. We use punishment for retaliation: "That'll teach 'em!"

We punish because we don't know what else to do. At least it is something. We are taking action, rather than feeling powerless. We get frustrated, angry. We are too stressed, too tired to think. It is easier to scold and threaten, which becomes its own punishment. I have been in homes where there is little real discipline but so much short temper, scolding, criticizing, ordering, and directing, with no joy, no fun, no laughter, that the parent and child seem locked into an atmosphere of unending punishment for both of them.

I remember a great cartoon from my childhood: a father has his child over his lap, bottom bared, hairbrush raised to strike. The caption: "This will teach you to hit people!"

That's one reason it is so important for you to take care of yourself. To safely let out all your anger and disappointment somewhere else than at the child. So you can think and decide how to take a more positive and effective approach.

We may even be unsure or doubtful about punishing, perhaps we force ourselves because the weight of our history and our culture impresses on us that it is necessary.

The problem is that control is impossible.

The control we seek is impossible.

You can't control people. Not in the long run. Perhaps you can make a threat that is strong enough to stop someone now, but that is not really control – as soon as the person is out of your range of influence he will do exactly as he pleases, not as you demand. Excessive punishment may work for a short time with a few people – but pickpockets continued to work the crowds that watched thieves being hanged. Sometimes dictatorships last a generation – but they all fall. It is going to be easier, more effective and more fun if you decide to give up controlling.

Punishment disconnects the bond. It creates a power struggle, turns an ally into an enemy. Parents try to explain their punishing: "I'm doing this for your own good." "I only do it because I love you." "This will help you learn." "This hurts me more than it does you." Did any of that ever make sense to you when you were young?

There is a Better Way

The Circle Way is how I think of it, having seen it in action in traditional native communities as well as in intentional communities where connection, respect for young people, and rituals of thanksgiving are part of daily life.

Connection, you could call it, understanding that disconnection, isolation, is the atmosphere we breathe, from which we develop our feelings and responses to the world.

So let us think about this again: what is it that a child needs?

You know, besides nourishment, exercise, health, safety, beyond the basic survival stuff. Children need what we all need.

A child needs to feel wanted, to belong, to be connected, to be appreciated, to be known and understood for who she is. A child needs information about herself and about the world. A child needs to like himself and to know he is liked and loved by others.

A child also needs to discover and learn about life and things for himself or herself.

But growing up doesn't need to be a struggle, a tug-of-war against restrictions and demands. It can be a dance. The kind you can watch in a toddler. She crawls or toddles away to explore. Looks back to see if someone is watching, comes back for re-assurance, toddles away further, explores something new. Perhaps brings something back to show. Finds approval, learns something more, and is off again. Adventures into the unknown, comes back to comfort and security.

This is the dance of life, and the young person will repeat it at every stage in different ways if there is a good connection at home, exploring further through school, through friends, through puberty and adolescence to adulthood. In our isolating society the bonds of parenthood and family are soon strained and frayed and weakened, and too often lost altogether. Family therapy is a major need of our time.

The Circle Way is the way human beings became human. The human being still develops his innate cooperativeness, helpfulness, kindness and compassion through closeness. Closeness in our dependent infancy with a mother, and hopefully with a father as well, and to other members of a close family, siblings, grandparents, aunts, uncles, cousins. And in the best traditional native communities this closeness can continue within a clan and a whole village.

In the old language of my people there was no separate word for "I" or "me", it was the same word as "we" or "us". We are our people, our people are us.

Ask a traditional Dine who he is and he will tell you the clan he was born to, his mother's clan, his father's clan, his family name, his village, and his nation. That's who he is.

The circle was created by our ancestors not just for protection, not just to survive, but to make life better for everyone. So the essence of the circle is closeness, cooperation, and helpfulness.

The help and the learning a child of a village following the circle way comes not only from papa and mama and the immediate family, but from the old and the young of the whole community. Since it is unlikely you would be reading this if you were now living in such a circle community, I will share what I have learned about developing such help for ourselves and our children in the last two chapters.

The first part of considering connection starts before the birth of a child. It concerns the connection and cooperation of the mother and father-to-be. The all-important subject of a couple's connection is not within our scope here, perhaps I may address that in another book. The bonding of mother and child will have begun *in utero* and from the moment of birth the enhancement and growth of that bond is in the best interest of both of them, as well as of the family and community – and of the whole world. It will be of first importance in the health and well-being of the child, and in the joy and the understanding of the mother, the family and the community.

At every stage the child will benefit from the love and the knowledge of her mother. This will be especially helpful during the growth spurts and social confusions of puberty and adolescence. So many of our young people are trying to pilot themselves through those turbulent waters alone because that bond is not strong enough for them to trust their parents and they are left to sort their way through the confusions of their peers.

I am hoping for every mother that she may have the understanding and cooperation of the father or some other caring adult able to give support and be included in this bond of trust. All the members of the family can be included in this bond of love and helpfulness. Siblings who also feel special and equally valued can also feel connected, that the baby is his or her little brother or sister who will need their help and of whom they may be proud.

The focus for parents, family, and community should not be on obedience or obligation, on following directions and rules, but on the quality of the relationships. And that depends on trust and communication, on understanding and being understood, and in the joys found together, having fun, being close, and affirming each other.

Children need to belong, to be connected, what they need is not a severing of the bond, not isolation or abandonment. More than ever they need our love and understanding – the best we can muster.

A Stranger in a Strange Land

The child is a newcomer. He doesn't know the customs and *mores* of your people yet. How would you guide and teach a stranger, a foreign visitor?

You don't want a child who just follows the rules because you told him to. Or because they are the rules. That's the attitude that let people send other people to concentration camps. Because they were told to. Because those were the rules.

We want children who will be able to make good decisions on their own, when we are not there with our rules and restrictions, our lectures and criticisms – to which they have long turned off their receptors. We want them to develop respect – which they only learn by being respected and seeing us respect others. We want them to be compassionate and understanding of others, which grows when they are treated with compassion and understanding. We want them to be confident and self-assured, which is enhanced by our appreciating them.

None of those are encouraged when children feel bad about themselves. They can regret and feel sorry for hurtful things they have done and still think of themselves as good and valuable people, especially when we can help them learn and resolve to act with better information, clearer thinking, or more compassion in the future. Jean Liedloff reports that among the Yequana a child is never told he is bad, or that he is always doing wrong. "He never feels he is bad, only, at most, that he is a loved child doing an undesirable act." She says that the child himself wants to stop doing anything that is distasteful to his people, and she comments ruefully that "real joy, the state in which the Yequana spend much of their lives, is exceedingly rare among us."

Rather than being their prosecutor, jury, judge, and warden, we want to be their guide, their counselor, their advocate and ally. We want to help them understand themselves and the pitfalls of life, to develop self-control and problem-solving skills.

For this we need to be connected to them. Punishment disconnects. Forced compliance builds barriers between us. Punishment hurts and so the intention confuses – it does not seem helpful. It creates defiance, anger, rebellion or passive aggression, breaks communication, and rewards lying. Both child and adult feel misunderstood.

Instead of punishment we need to be facilitating closeness, which means communication, which means listening. More listening and less lecturing. Remember the first time you tell a child something it is information, perhaps the second time it may only be a reminder – if we then listen to the child's reaction, but the third time and all times after that it's just another lecture.

Helping children with their learning, their self-discipline, their physical health, their emotional well being, their relations with others, all work best with a good connection. A strong emotional connection. Whether a parent, grandparent, sibling, teacher, doctor, counselor, or friend, the ones who have meant the most to us and affected our lives the most are the ones we loved the most.

You don't like to be bossed. None of us likes it. We don't want to live in a family or a country with a dictator. You don't go to a doctor you don't trust, who doesn't listen to you and talk to you but only gives directions. We only accept direction and advice from people we trust. The more we trust them the more we accept from them. Trust comes from closeness, from love, from mutual understanding and appreciation.

So of course it is best and easiest if the initial emotional bond between the adult and child that begins with mother and baby and may be extended later to others, it is easiest if that bond of trust, caring and understanding is not ever broken. But what if it has? What if there is no trust on which to base a discipline created by both child and adult together? What if the child is not your own? How to create trust with a community member, a student, patient or client?

It is still possible and eminently advisable instead of punishment to create closeness and trust and participate together in coming to an understanding and mutually acceptable way of working together.

The tool is the same: listening. A lot of listening. Listening and understanding. Being assured of the understanding by checking with the child and then working together to plan what steps will most benefit the needs of the child.

We want to raise children who feel like participants, not victims. Even rules that must be imposed, like no hitting, no playing on the highway, and so on, need to be accepted. Which means different things at different ages, but from the time they are old enough to question a rule they should be listened to well and responded to in the attitude of thinking together, exploring and participating in finding mutual understanding and agreement. Of course agreements may and will be broken sometimes. The consequence, to be effective, must not be punitive but a further participation and exploration to find a solution that is mutually acceptable.

Here I would like to refer you again to the work of Dr. Thomas Gordon, who says there are three basic styles of relating to children: the first being the adult gives the orders and the child must obey; the second being the child is basically in charge and does what he wants. Neither of these works well. The third way we used in our community and called "working it out." In this way the child and the adult use problem solving to find a no-lose solution that both can agree to. This process worked well for all of us, even when the children were pre-verbal and could just accept or reject a proposal with a head movement. Further detail can be found in Gordon's books (See the bibliography).

What about the method sometimes called "consequences"? What about "time out"? What about "rewards?" Are they good replacements for punishment?

My take on "consequences" is that they are not real consequences, the natural, inevitable reaction to the behavior. They are invented and imposed consequences, and children can see through that ruse quickly and judge these consequences for what they actually are: punishment.

Time Out

About "time out" – is that a punishment? Depends, I would say. I think it is often used punitively – and taken as a punishment in the child's estimation. But I also think there are times when we adults need a break. We aren't relaxed, we are tense, feeling rigid and responding too quickly, curtly, brusquely, getting irritated. *We* need a time out. I suggest you leave whatever was irritating and do something more fun. For you both. Together if you can, but separately if that feels easier for the time. Refresh yourself. Maybe call a friend and discharge and re-think your approach to the issue. Then go bring it up again and listen. "Time out" too often is only a contemporary euphemism for "go sit in the corner" or "stay in your room until you can behave."

Rewards

About "rewards". If you think about it, rewards have many of the same negative effects that punishment has. Instead of making us the enemy, they make us the prize-givers. They don't make the children feel closer to us or more understanding of us. They are not complying with us because they agree or understand but only for payment. And if payment is withheld, that feels like punishment to them. We are further isolated, and we are encouraging the consumer ethic, that value resides in material wealth and possessions, not in affection and closeness and the fun of doing things together.

Connection Instead of Control

I will probably say this again somewhere in this book, but to remember the basic activities and attitudes recommended here you could perhaps simplify it to only two words.

Two words:

Listen…and hug.

Listening being the activity of trying to understand the child, whether she is talking or laughing, or crying, or screaming, or running, jumping, dancing, throwing, hitting, or just sitting or standing in a certain posture, looking with a certain facial expression.

Hugging being affection – appreciating and showing your love whether by a word of praise, by a hug, a pat on the back, a ruffling of the hair, a squeeze of the hand, a cheer, a gasp, or even just an approving smile.

Listening is the default position we need always to return to when we are confused or conflicted, or when things are not working well.

Hugs are the best medicine where at any time we can let go,

express our joy in the gifts of life and love, and the wonderful children we get to hang out with.

Even though you really cannot control any human being in the long run, you absolutely can and must set limits for children under your care, for their health and safety and for our own sanity and peace of mind. The next chapter will address that need.

Chapter Nine
Setting Limits

"Permissive child raising leaves children stuck in distress by themselves."

–Tim Jackins

I was driving on one of our backcountry New Hampshire roads, and a local police officer pulled me over for being a bit in excess of the speed limit.

"What's the hurry?" he asked. "I'm sorry," I said, "but it's Friday and my computer is waiting at the repair shop that closes at six o'clock."

The officer told me to wait, went back to his car, then returned and told me to go on and not speed – he had called the store and they would wait for me, so I could take my time.

Have you ever had the police stop you for an infraction, listen to your story, and let you go with a warning? You feel so grateful, so glad for friendly and understanding treatment by an authority whose job it is, you realize, to keep everyone safe. We don't like authority, but when we have to have it, we want to feel like it's on our side.

If, however, you ever get a cop in a bad mood, who is annoyed by your explanation, lectures you, you may feel unfairly treated, even though the ticket you get is absolutely justified. You think more about not getting caught than about changing your driving habits. Attitude of the enforcer contributes a great deal to our thought and behavior about authority.

We adults are the enforcers of the rules of the children in our care. How we do that strongly affects our relationships with them, and their feelings and behavior towards us. Through the manner in which we enforce the rules we influence their feelings. Will those feelings be ones of trust and closeness and openness? Or ones of mistrust, distance, and hiding.

Of course we have this role, it is necessary for their health and safety. It is necessary for their emotional well being – and ours.

Children do better when limits are clear and understood. At various times they will try to push those limits and cross over the borders. We all did that, remember? But they need to know that we care and will hold to those limits.

So setting limits is vitally important. And it's important to hold those limits in a way that maintains understanding and trust between us and the child and encourages their confidence in themselves.

Attitude, therefore, is extremely important here. Gentle but firm is the slogan. That's what this whole chapter will be about. How to stay firm, keep the necessary and reasonable limits that are set, and in keeping them staying always calm, understanding and caring. A tall order? Well – at first maybe, but it gets easier with practice, and with a little help from our friends – (see Chapter Eleven).

Sometimes it's like, "Friends don't let friends drive drunk" – you take the keys and let them swear at you as you smile and say "Come on, buddy, I'll drive you home." They are not themselves, you have to be in charge, but you don't want to hurt them. You physically prevent them from hurting anyone and try to stay patient and understanding.

You know whenever you have to prevent anyone from doing anything he is going to get upset. But you must not let that upset you. What do you do when people are upset? If you have come this far in this book you will know the answer: you listen to them.

When you have to set a limit and stop a child from doing something, you know ahead of time they will be upset. So you are prepared to listen as they pour out their upset on you. You show that you are listening and that you care how they feel, and you let them know you understand them, and still you must hold the limit. Don't argue, don't explain, they won't hear if they are upset, if they don't stop when you say stop, just prevent them, do whatever it takes, gently, physically, to restrain them.

With a baby, naturally, there is no explaining. She will understand your action but not your words. You might say "no-no" – but I would caution you about that. Babies hear a lot of "no-no." They learn the meaning of that faster than anything. "Yes" as a word is learned much later because it is not heard nearly as much. If you can, only gently and physically prevent the immediate danger or harm. Hug, or pick up the child, take her attention to something else, remove the dangerous or fragile object out of reach without a "no-no." The action will speak for itself, and the child will understand eventually – better to limit the "no-nos" to a few. They will then have more power and coherence.

But "no-no" or not, the limiting adult needs to stay light and happy with the baby, playful, maybe funny too. Limiting can be done with humor; it can be done with singing. The gentleness of the touch, the warmth of embrace, the hugs, the kisses, the smile of pleasure and joy, the tones of love, these are what are most important.

Of course, that's not always that easy for us, and the difficulty will increase with the increasing age of the child. A baby is sweet and helpless and brings out the caretaker and nurturer in us – until they get colic or some unknown distress and scream for hours inconsolably. At which we are liable to get frazzled and frantic and need help ourselves.

I hope, if you are caring for an infant, that you have the help you need. One very good way to use that help we have described in earlier chapters – that is to share sessions where you get to let out all your feelings and then make good decisions about how you approach the problems (and also joys) of being with the child. You will find more about creating such help for yourself in Chapter Eleven.

The older the child gets the more of a challenge he will be to your composure, your calm and reasonable responses, your understanding and firm limit-setting during his outbursts of energy, of aggressiveness, of whining and shouting, screaming and tantrums. They are all so sweet and lovable, when they sleep!

One point I want to stress is preparation. Knowing that setting limits will almost surely evoke opposition and emotional turmoil, you need to prepare yourself for that. Get a session where you think and express feelings about setting limits with this child. Rehearse staying calm in the face of whining and wheedling, anger, quiet manipulation – "you're a terrible mother!" – threats, promises, tears, sullen shutting down – be ready.

"Hurt feelings confine a child to unloving, fearful, or inflexible behavior, which is a clear request for help. A child who is upset or inflexible will recover from his feelings of hurt if a caring adult moves in warmly and listens while he discharges his upset."

–Patty Wipfler

Remember the short version of this book – the two words that sum up the instruction at any point – hug and listen. Show in facial expression, vocal tones, body language, and words that you deeply care for this little person, and listen to her. Listen with all your heart as she pours out her grief or anger to you. Let her know you have heard and that you really, really understand and appreciate her, but that the limit has to be upheld.

Two things can help here. Beginning when a child's cognitive powers can comprehend and respond, you can allow a greater amount of choice and power to them, and I heartily endorse that. The more we can help our babies become active participants in their world, the more skillful, competent, and confident they become. Studies show, for instance, that babies who are fed on demand, when they are asking for it, become more competent and intelligent than babies who are fed on a schedule. Because they are feeling part of the process, having an effect on their own lives. The process of childhood is about children developing their power, and it helps our children when we give opportunities for them to do that.

Our power comes from our ability to choose. When we have no choice we feel powerless, hopeless, and tend to get depressed. But we always have a choice. When we remember that, our confidence and optimism returns. We can choose where we will put our attention, we can choose how we will react. Remember Reinhold Niebuhr's Serenity Prayer that we have the power to change the things that can be changed, the serenity to accept what cannot be changed, and the wisdom to know the difference.

The more choices we are able to give our children, the more alert and engaged they remain. By our holding firm to the limits they eventually are able to accept them, especially if there is some choice also available. My sons are both remarkable teachers of this way. I have listened to them again and again with children and marveled at their patience, thinking to myself they had the advantage of their parent's mistakes and strengths, encouragement and faith to stand upon. At least Emmy and I listened and encouraged their expression of the feelings and the thinking of both our sons.

Tokeem, my older boy, would inform his son Linus that he could not do something now that the boy really wanted to do. Then he would offer a couple of alternatives that Linus could choose.

"No!" Linus would say, "I want…"

"You really want to do that now, Linus, I understand. I'm sorry that isn't possible, but – " then Tokeem would repeat the offer, sometimes perhaps adding another alternative to choose from.

"Never!" Says Linus – for a while that became his favorite word. He has spirit, my grandson. And they would keep it up. Tokeem always calm and understanding, light in his tone but firm in the limit. Linus would try everything but finally realized that he was confronting one of the things that cannot be changed and he would choose one of the alternatives offered.

It takes time, and great patience, a lot of listening and responding in an understanding way, with lightness and sympathy and a bit of friendly humor and playfulness. If you understand that there will probably be resistance to the limit, you will do well to think this out well ahead of time, to allow plenty of time for the child to make a choice, so you don't have to carry him kicking and screaming because you are already late.

The old way, traditional in Europe and in many cultures, may seem so much easier: "You do what I say now, and don't talk back!" But in actuality it is not easier. It builds up distance, walls, resentment, and either submission that reduces the child's involvement, confidence and creativity, or rebellion that undermines his confidence in you. A little investment of time and patience in giving choices bears wonderful fruit in cooperation and joy in your times together.

Even if the child makes a choice there might be a lingering regret about the limit. It is good to stay connected, to talk about it and listen, and eventually turn the attention to subjects of livelier interest and more fun. When we are accepting of them, of all their feelings and thoughts, and we show we like them and enjoy the time together, children also want the time to be fun. Another good time to offer choices – or just be really silly.

As children's cognitive skills grow they may want to question the limits that have been or are to be set. Good. Another step in learning to think together, to listen and be listened to, to give and receive respect. *Parent Effectiveness Training* (P.E.T.) was congenial to our mutual desire for complete respect for the personhood of every child, so Emmy and I used it with our children and taught it to others.

All the children in our community knew the system well and might use it with each other even if no adult were present to help. When outsiders visited our community and tried to tell our children what to do in the old authoritarian manner, our children would tell them that's not the way things worked there, they had to "work it out" with them, and if they didn't know how to do that the children were willing to teach them.

Conflict Resolution

In that system, as in all conflict resolution, the first step is to identify the problem. When there is a conflict it is probable that those affected may all have a different view of what the problem is. So that needs to be looked at and discussed. Whose problem is this? When that has been clarified, for the next step everyone involved, adult or child, is encouraged to make suggestions about solving the problem. It could help to take time and come up with a variety of suggestions. Humor can help here, fanciful and funny solutions that make everyone relax and laugh. The last step is picking a solution that could be agreed to by all. A solution in which one party wins and another loses is not going to work. What is needed here is a "no-lose" solution.

The children in our community got very good at working it out. They came up with many very creative solutions. One time there was an outbreak of fighting among the children that seemed suddenly to be occurring every day. The children realized they were not able to solve it and asked for help. We had a circle with all the children and a few adults, and everyone listened to each other.

We adults made no suggestions, only appreciated and encouraged the young people in their process. The decision of the children ultimately was to have a daily pillow fight in the Great Hall of the community which was amply provided with dozens of cushion. The battle would also be mandatory for everyone on the premises at the time. Once a day all the children trouped through the house and grounds announcing the fray. For one hour the air of the Great Hall was filled with flying cushions and laughing people. The adults loved this time-out for wild exercise and chaotic uncontrolled joy, the young ones gleefully relished the safe time to expend all their pent-up energy on blasting grown-ups, delighting in their power. And there were no more fights among the children.

The process of working out no-lose solutions can begin even before babies are capable of expressing their wishes verbally. An adult who knows the process and understands the child can suggest what she believes the problem to be from the child's point of view in words the child can comprehend. The child will be able to indicate agreement or disagreement with a nod or a shake of the head. The adult can then offer several solutions, and if all are rejected keep trying, perhaps getting fanciful and silly, introducing fun and play.

When an agreement is reached, a solution that the child accepts which works for the adult too, the adult needs to make sure it is carried out as agreed, and reviews afterward with child what the agreement was and how well it worked and if it needed new thinking. Also noting how much fun it was to work out such things together. As children experience that choices are available to them, that they have the ability to make them, they get better at the process and at thinking and being creative about solutions.

The second ingredient, an all-important one not covered in the P.E.T. process, that Emmy and I began to learn and teach from our training in Re-evaluation Counseling, was in our understanding about emotions. Much of what I read and hear from teachers about relating to children has to do with how to be rational, to help children use their good thinking in their relationships, in what they choose, in how they look at the world. Very important, all of that. But I read and hear very little about the crucial area of children's feelings.

In the earlier chapters of this book you have read how central it is to our caring for children that we understand and know how to effectively handle their feelings – and also our own. In the next chapter I will go into the subject of strong emotions more fully.

What we need to keep in mind about setting limits is that children will not always welcome limits and setting them may arouse very strong feelings. We need to be prepared for that. If they are already doing something dangerous or hurtful they may need to be physically restrained and that may infuriate them. If we have to take something from them they may be angry or grief-stricken. We must move into mode of sympathetic listening to their rage or sorrow. Not try to stop or divert it, but listen and show we hear them and we understand their feelings. Everyone's emotions need expression – it is part of the healing process. When the overwhelming power of the emotion has an outlet we are soon relieved and able to think more clearly about the whole situation. We can view it in a new light and make new choices to deal with it in a way that might be beneficial. When there is a caring and understanding listener it makes it easier for us to release them. We should encourage them in the expression of their feelings, not contradict them, not try to change them, but show we are glad that they share them with us.

A wonderful thing about children in general is that they have not had as much time as we have to repress spontaneous expressions and pretend the feelings don't affect us when they have only been driven underground. After we have succeeded in receiving the outburst with understanding, we may then be able to help the child find options and choices that give her a greater sense of power and freedom within the limits. The child learns there are things you can change and things you can't – that's how life is – but you can do a lot with what you can change.

There may come times when you must instantly stop a child from what he is doing. With a baby no words are needed, just the immediate interruption, restraining physically but calmly, gently, with no anger or upset, maybe with a song or a playful diversion. With an older child the interruption should be quick and physical at once, no screaming "What are you doing? You should know better! What's the matter with you?" Keep anything you need to say brief and simple: "I can't let you do that." An explanation at that point will seem like a lecture and be tuned out – or argued with. A short statement may prevent argument: "We don't do that in this house," "It's not okay to hit," "That hurts."

Your physical restraint may bring about physical retaliation. You have to be ready for that too. Remember to be as gentle as is possible, to use only as much force as is necessary to restrain, to not get angry, to not say the child is bad, only that this behavior is not allowed. Then be prepared for much discharge of feelings, crying, fighting, kicking, biting, screaming, swearing. Here it is best not to get upset yourself, but stay calm and listen to the feelings while holding the limit. Don't talk a lot, just a few words to let them know you aren't angry: "I like you a lot – but I can't let you do that." Make your restraint as loving as the situation allows while keeping the child from hitting, scratching, biting, kicking you, and respond to their curses on you lightly and with affectionate humor.

During all that you want to stay centered and calm. How? Well, my method is to keep talking to myself, reminding myself this is a wonderful child that is being controlled by feelings he cannot handle, that the feelings are not his fault, that he really wants to be rid of them and this is the best way he knows to do that. I think it is probable that he began this behavior to draw attention to feelings he didn't understand that were eating at him, in the hopes that he would find a way to discharge them so he could be his own funny, fun-loving sweet self again. Perhaps he really hopes I can help somehow even though he is fighting me. I remind myself that I am stronger and I know this will come out well and he will eventually get all this out and we will be close because he will understand that I love him and was doing all I could to help him.

Setting Limits – A Session

We were at the end of a weekend workshop we were giving a varied assortment of people from many countries who happened to be staying at a small island center. There was a five-year-old boy there whom I will call Tommy, bright and energetic and full of life – and mischief. Unfortunately the center had not expected or prepared for children at the workshop, their care was left up to the parents who wanted to devote their attention to the workshop, and the children were told to "go and play." This was not meeting Tommy's needs and he constantly sought attention from the adults. What attention he got from his young single mother was mostly an attempt to try and control him in his fleeting assaults on people. I liked Tommy. A lot. I thought his wild forays were often imaginative and humorous, but also provocative and sometimes unwanted – especially by the other little boy his age who complained about him.

I wanted to take some time to give him attention, to play with him and let him use me to express and let go of the demons that demanded our notice. But this was not a family workshop, and as he was not disrupting the participants during the circles I thought I would wait until the workshop ended.

Fate – or Tommy – hastened that decision at the end of the final circle. Tommy began hitting the smaller boy and, as always, laughed and ran away, laughing again at his mother as she tried to grab him but he was too fleet for her.

I had been watching this develop, as we all had when he began hitting the protesting boy. I thought to myself, "All right, Tommy, you have been showing us all what you need, so I guess it's time now for me to help you with that."

I was out of my chair quickly and was right there when he danced away from his mother. I reached around from behind him and snatched his left wrist with my right hand as I grabbed his right wrist with my left, and I hugged him to me, his back pressed to the front of my body, lifting him swiftly and backed us both up to my chair and sat with him on my lap. At first he laughed – it was a game and he was getting the attention he wanted at last. Then he tried to get away, but I held on, firmly but gently, using my embrace to immobilize the struggle of his arms, avoiding his attempts to kick me with his feet or butt me with his head. He shouted at me to let go, and I stayed calm, not angry or upset, telling him in a soft and friendly tone, "I'm not going let go, I'm just going to hold you until you calm down. I'm not going to let you hit anyone."

He screamed in indignation and anger for me to release him and used over and over the limited number of foul words he had acquired in his short life. I just kept telling him, in a light and pleasant voice, "I like you Tommy, I really do. But I am not going to let you go now while you are still so angry." And I hugged him closer and nuzzled him playfully.

"Let me go," he shouted, "I hate you! I'm going to kill you!"

"Well then," still very lightly, I said, "I guess I better not let you go then, I don't want to be killed!"

And so it went for about forty-five minutes. The circle, at first interested, then concerned, began trying to get him to understand, but I told them that while he is so upset there is no point in trying to reason with him – he could not hear it through his anger. And I could feel it in his body, that he wanted to join the laughter – a little piece of his mind worked for just an instant, but he still had more strength and energy left for the struggle.

In all that time I kept reminding myself that his physical struggle was just what he needed and really wanted. His actions had really been a cry for help without his awareness or conscious intention. He didn't know what to do with all those wild aggressive feelings pressing inside him except to rage and fight, and he needed to do it in a safe way that wouldn't hurt him or anyone else. I had to tell myself that, as old as I was, he was having to put out much more energy fighting than I was holding, and I could outlast him and give him the opportunity to discharge all that stuff boiling inside him. I reminded myself what a wonderful little boy he was, and how I admired the warrior in him that wouldn't give up, and that the distresses eating him were not his fault, not anyone's fault. That my holding him, my physical closeness, and my liking him and pulling for him were things he wanted and needed.

In fact, I started to feel that he was beginning to accept the challenge of this struggle as something he could use, something he needed.

Eventually of course he did get tired, and his mind started to click on to figure out how he could get out of this. I could feel that in him – I had done this so many times with so many children in my life – and it always works.

"I'll stop if you will," he said.

"Okay, Tommy. I'll let you go if you can make an agreement with me."

A big change. Now he was curious. I watched him really thinking.

"What's that?"

"You have to agree to stop hitting people, that's all. But you have to really mean it and really do it. I believe you can do that."

He thought again for a moment.

"Not even my mother?"

"No, Tommy, not even your mother. Hitting hurts." He thought again.

"All right."

I set him down and he broke loose instantly and ran. We all watched to see what he would do next.

He ran around behind the circle, running to every person, one at a time, most of them strangers to him, and he hugged every one, a big strong hug for each.

When he came to me, the last one, he hugged me from behind

shyly at first, then without letting go worked his way around to crawl up onto my lap, put his head on my chest, hugging hard, and crying. By now I was crying too, and so were most of the circle. And then he fell asleep.

From that time on, for the rest of that evening and the next day on the long boat ride to the mainland, Tommy never left my side. He snuggled, he played and laughed with me, as if he had known me forever and it was the most natural thing in the world. And so it was. The absolutely natural way that people could always be with one another if they have no confusing distressful feelings but are relaxed and open to enjoy each other.

That was almost two years ago and I have seen Tommy since and played with him, though he does not speak much English and I do not speak his language we are comfortable with each other, and his mother says he is quite a transformed little boy, that she and all of us had a great lesson that day on the island.

Part Four

"It is possible that the next Buddha will not take the form of an individual. The next Buddha may take the form of a community – a community practicing understanding and loving kindness, a community practicing mindful living. This may be the most important thing we can do for the survival of the Earth."

–Thich Nhat Hanh

Chapter Ten
The Circle Way

"The first purpose of the circle was to help the people, and the first purpose of the people was to help the circle."
—Manitonquat

You have perhaps wondered just what is this "Circle Way" referred to in the title of this book. The Circle Way is the way many of us have begun to figure out how to adapt the best of what human beings developed over more than ten millennia of living together on our Earth. For me that includes all I have been taught by many wise elders of First Nations and have learned from native parents trying to raise their children in traditional ways throughout North America. Also what I have been able to pick up from talking to indigenous elders and young people from every continent, whom I have met in many gatherings, and from correspondence with them while I was an editor of the native journal *Akwesasne Notes*. I conveyed this information to the circles of the small community we created in New Hampshire in the 1970s, and to the family workshops and camps we have been developing for over thirty years.

The Oglala holy man Nick Black Elk said that everything our people do we do in a circle because the power of the world works in circles. If we extend our concept of the circle to include sphere, ovals, ellipses and spirals, that would seem to be true. He noted that when we were a strong and happy people all our power came from the sacred circle of the people. In that concept of the circle was the belief that all things are connected and all things are sacred. The Creation is alive, and all life, all beings, all people are connected and sacred. So the children are sacred, the women, the men, the elders, all equally important and sacred, and the circle of all of them, the nations, the communities and clans, were all equally sacred and important for they weave the web of life for the people. In the thinking and concern of the people the circle was paramount. The circle derives its power from the spirit that connects all, and the thinking and concern of the circle was for each person, child, woman, man, and elder, and that gave them their strength. The first purpose of the circle was to help the people, and the first purpose of the people was to help the circle.

Any position that a person held in the community was not for the power or the honor of holding the position, as those things tend to get in the way of the purpose of that position, which was to serve and be helpful. People found joy not in accumulating or owning, but in being and connecting – with each other, with children and elders, with the plant and animal life, with wind, water, Earth, sun, moon and stars.

Because children bring out the tenderness of people, because connection with them is a joy, tenderness and joy are their gifts.

At some time in their lives many if not most people will seek meaning – the meaning of their existence. Why are we here? What is it we are meant to contribute? In the middle of a successful and gratifying career in the theater I felt I needed a better answer to those questions. The world needed a better response from me. So after twelve exciting years doing what I relish and do best, I left the theater and after some searching began to find elders who spoke to me of the Original Instructions for human beings and how they had been lost in this dominant colonizing culture. This changed my life, and I started to follow a new path, to learn and share how a human being might follow these instructions in the light of modern knowledge and the social conditions of today.

The ideal picture I have drawn of life in the circle is not the whole story – it is only the best of it. There have been places and circles in our history where practices have grown into traditions and stagnated, limiting thinking and blocking growth out of piety and fear. But when the respect the elders insisted upon has been maintained, where the thinking and creativity of all have been attended to and honored – especially that of the children – it enhanced the strength and resilience, as well as the thoughtfulness, the compassion, kindness and joy in the life of the people.

Black Elk also noted that the sacred circle of his people had been shattered by the conquerors, and it broke his heart. But after his death in the early 1950s, his prayers and his vision for his nation and for the Earth began to stir and become known to a new generation to raise the spirits of all native people to find their way back to the sacred circle.

My studies in anthropology have shown me that it was the circle that made us into human beings, that caring for the children for the many years it takes for a human child to become an full-grown adult, made us tender and compassionate, and encouraged us to extend for all our lives the curiosity and wonder, the playfulness and joy of childhood.

As a teacher, educator and creator of schools, a participant in conscious community building, a leader of family workshops and camps, and as a father and a grandfather, my experiences have only supported these beliefs while honing the tools we create to implement them. So, since we all want children to grow into their full potentials, here follow some thoughts oriented to the Circle Way about four areas of a full human being. (I tend to organize my thinking in fours, in the native way as my elders often thought, such as in the four seasons and the four cardinal directions.)

North – Direction of Body

The first part to consider is the physical aspect. This would include our providing a safe and healthy environment for ourselves and our loved ones, and we would understand that to expand outward to include a safe and healthy neighborhood, community, nation and planet. We would want only the healthiest food, clean and pure water and air, sufficient exercise and play, rest and sleep, to keep our families fit, and available medical care as might be required. Each of these things are topics that a family as well as a community might think about and discuss with children, including the children's thoughts while decisions are made.

What we do not need and most of us have already too much of are material possessions. We are cluttering our lives with stuff and confusing our children as well as ourselves with too many toys and gadgets. We derive so much more pleasure from the material world when we do not acquire and own and amass collections of junk. Advertising, catalogues, shopping centers are tantalizing us into excesses that are touted to bring us satisfaction or pleasure which perhaps they may for a few hours before they go on a shelf or in a closet or attic. Our children derive more pleasure from the boxes toys come in than from the toys themselves. When we rid ourselves of stuff at a yard sale, we feel purified and relieved – until the next sale or catalogue arrives. We read Thoreau and determine to simplify – would we come closer to ourselves and life in a humble cabin in the woods of Walden?

Connection is important in order to escape the isolation and loneliness of our culture, and physical touch is important in making and maintaining those connections. Friendly hugs, cuddling, patting, wrestling, sitting on laps all feel good to children and to all of us. Once long ago I visited a community in the Trinity Alps of California where, in the morning, everyone gathered to brush each other's hair, adults and children, men and women. It was a warm and comforting ritual enjoyed by all.

East – Direction of Mind

The second direction concerns the mind, the mental aspect. The primary instruction in children, built in to every developing cell, is to grow and to learn. Everything for them is about learning, their play, their fun, their explorations, their observations, their expressions. They learn an amazing amount in the early years of life, how to control their bodies, to control their hands and fingers, legs and feet, bladders and bowels, learning a whole language, how to speak and read and write. They will learn quickly because they want to, and engage themselves fully in that learning. When we try to teach them things, we are too often apt to interfere with that desire to learn. For them learning is fun, and when they are free to follow their interests and have fun they are great learners, but when it stops being fun, when we are imposing it in a way that is too fast and confusing or too slow and boring, or too harsh, they lose interest and the desire to learn wilts. John Holt used to say that if we attempted to teach children to speak the way we try to teach them to read they would take much longer – years perhaps – to learn to speak. There in a nutshell is what is wrong with our educational systems. They are not geared to make any of the subjects fun, and they restrict the free ranging of the children's interests.

We don't have to worry so much about developing our children's minds. If we can make resources available, and if we use those resources ourselves, they will use them. They want to explore. They are very inquisitive. If we read ourselves and we read to them, if we go to the library and explore with them there, if we research with them our questions in dictionaries, encyclopedias and the Internet, they will pursue their interests and acquire a life-long habit of learning.

My mother read to me regularly. She loved books and literature – the center of our home was the library. She discussed books and films with me, and listened as I related to her in detail the plots of every story. She gave me books as presents and took me to movies and the theater. When I discovered an old Caruso record of her mother's, my mother, being herself unmusical and knowing nothing of music, bought me, on recommendation of a store clerk, a record of Brahms fifth and sixth Hungarian Dances. Thereby she incited in me a lifelong passion to listen and learn all I could about great music of every kind. And that has enriched my life more than any other single pursuit.

In my grandmother's parlor was an old baby grand piano, a gift of my grandfather who passed away before I was born. I was told she used to play and sing beautifully, but I never heard her. The grown-ups all gathered in her library upstairs, and the parlor was left unattended, a museum piece. I was of course magnetically pulled to those alluring ivory keys, and sat at them for hours on end, alone relishing the sounds I could make with them. From the age of four I explored them whenever we visited my grandmother, who lived only a third of a mile from our house, and by the time I was in high school I had taught myself to play all the popular tunes of the day. All my life I have heard people tell me they wished they could play but their parents forced them to take boring lessons so they quit as soon as they could and never learned. I have since played in a dance band in the Army, sat in with a New Orleans jazz band and with various rock groups in the 60s and 70s, while playing for my supper at restaurants up and down the Pacific Coast, and for three years played in New Hampshire with a local band every week, covering oldies from that earlier rock era.

Curiosity, the desire and the ability to learn are innate in every human being. If we only expose children to the wonders of our world and the possibilities to explore and discover them, they want to learn. What hampers them is making them sit for hours every day with a lot of other children subjected to nothing curious or exciting or relevant to their interests – an hour of mathematics, an hour of history, an hour of biology – and so on, only memorizing and regurgitating what they are told. It doesn't end at their release in the afternoon but returns in homework to steal more of the precious hours of childhood, and looming over all the fear and humiliation of testing and grading, killing any possibility of joy and delight in discovering the wonders of the world.

One of the best classes I had in high school was one year in biology – not because of the subject – I don't remember any of that – but our teacher was a last minute replacement for the science teacher, one who was himself an English teacher. He didn't even try to teach us the text. Instead we went on field trips every day to observe nature. Imagine! No books, no blackboard, no lecture. We all walked through the woods, the fields and the shoreline of the river. We observed the flowers and the trees, the birds and the dragonflies; we marveled at the great web of life. I have forgotten all the other courses and their texts, but I still remember those field trips.

Another English teacher was a powerful influence on me at that time. A white-haired old man with twinkling eyes we all called "Chief". Chief took a liking to my writing compositions and encouraged me to indulge my fantasies and write my own stories rather than the assigned book reports. He advised me to write from my passions, whatever I really cared about. I was fired to excessive flights of sensuous detail that would no doubt embarrass me to read today – but that was certainly me in my early adolescence. Perhaps it still is.

Storytelling

Children love stories. We all love stories. They are the way human beings have passed knowledge and understanding from generation to generation from the earliest times. Children resist teaching and preaching – we all do – but they delight in stories and reach into their hearts for meaning, absorbed by the desire to explore and learn, and the needs for justice and the balancing of disharmonized forces.

My grandfather was a great storyteller. When he wanted to give me a lesson, in deportment or respect or tolerance, enlarging my consciousness of the world, he told a story. Sometimes a traditional story of our people, and sometimes a made-up homely tale of animals in the woods and fields and on the seashore. His stories are still alive in me, and one reason I write and tell them to people everywhere now.

The teachings that become so oppressive and boring in school come alive in us as we experience the adventures of others in a tale. The stories of Astrid Lindgren, for instance, nourish the hearts and minds of every Swedish child and many others in the world. Every little girl I know has been delighted and empowered by Pippi Longstocking.

As a solitary child I made stories for the many hand puppet characters I had, and for the small theater I later was given with many characters molded of lead. I also loved my mother reading to me nearly every night, and eagerly told my own stories on my daily rounds to our elderly neighbor Mrs. Waters, the Browns, a retired couple down the street, and my great-grandparents on the next street. Then came the wonderful worlds of radio that without the scenic display of today's television gave a free rein to the imagination.

In secondary school the most influential teacher of my young life, Francis Hyde Bangs, taught me to question everything that I was taught, every assertion in all I read, but also to read and ponder the living truths in the literature of all lands. We recall vividly the teachings of the world's spiritual traditions only because of their stories.

So, if you want any child to receive your truth I implore you – don't lecture, don't preach, don't even try to teach – tell a story.

South – Direction of Heart

The third direction is that of the heart. One of my favorite stories from my grandfather is that of First Man, who, when he asked his grandmother how to know what to do, was told "Follow your heart." When asked how to do that she told him to ask his heart, "what is the most loving thing I can do right now?" Love is at the center of the world's religions and philosophies, and the most popular theme of our fiction, popular music, film and television, psychotherapy and self-help books. We can't define it, don't agree about it, but we know it and feel it and long for it when it is absent. It is the very center of our being. People used to say it's what makes the world go round, and often "God is love." Meaning, I suppose, that the force of Creation guiding all existence is what we call love.

As famously stated by Erich Fromm, love is an art. Not an emotion, but an interpersonal creative capacity. We all have the potential for it when we are born. When we are loved it blooms in us, but when we are not, when the world is not made safe for us, we may not learn the art, reacting instead with fear or fury in order to survive. Speaking comes naturally to us, but to speak well we must study the art of speaking. We will love naturally wherever we are encouraged to and feel ourselves wanted, but to love well is also an art that can be learned: to love oneself, one's family and intimate friends, one's community, strangers, and enemies. Most of the religious texts and teachers tell us to love one another, but they do not teach us how.

I do not mean to imply that I am a master of this art. I am still a student. I see in myself what I must learn, and also how much I have learned of it in my 85 years. I can reflect on how much better I might have modeled that study for my children and how much more I exhibit now with all children including my grandchildren, and where I still fall short.

Sue Gerhardt writes, in her book *Why Love Matters,* that research shows all babies arrive seeking social interaction, and that the full development of their brains, their immune systems, their emotional intelligence, confidence and ability to regulate their feelings depend on the experience of caring adults who show interest in them and react positively to them. In other words, with love. She writes, "...we need to go back to the origins of emotional life, to the early processes which determine our emotional trajectories – to the baby and her emotional environment."

It is easier to do this with the very young, who learn and change so quickly. But in my experience, although it takes more time and attention to help a person to emotional stability the older he is, at every age the power of compassion, of listening and understanding, accepting and appreciating, will work its healing magic upon anyone. Children themselves can be our best healers in that as exemplified in the stories of Silas Marner and Little Lord Fauntleroy, where bitter old men were transformed by the innocence of a child.

Most of us do learn that we feel content and safe only when we feel truly loved for ourselves alone, for who we are. We learn it clearly when we are aware of the deprivation of love, of the emptiness of our nights and the longing of our days. We see it in the baby's anguish at mama's disappearance and in her joy in mama's return. As we grow through the world we believe that love is our due, what we were born for, and if we are not loved we should be – if love is withheld there is something very wrong, wrong with the world, or with other people, or with ourselves.

As we seek that love in our isolating culture, too often we are diverted to inadequate and even dangerous substitutions: to inappropriate lovers who mistreat themselves or us, to addictions to work, material wealth and possessions, notoriety, drugs. We see this lack of love in continual oppressions, warfare, genocide, and a greed-infected culture. It's depressing when one considers the splendor of human possibility. But often another pair of searching eyes may appreciate us and hope and beauty rise again before us – we reach out once more joyfully for the promise of love.

And when a child is born to us hope springs once more in our hearts. That little face turns up to us, those curious eyes hold us and we are in love. The little one is so tiny, so perfect, yet so helpless, and we sense an awe of being her connection to who she will become.

The baby is our teacher, stirring in us the essence of our being – our love, our need to help, to be trusted and needed ourselves, to give the gift of all we are and know. The bond that may be formed between us is a sacred one that binds us in mutual growth and learning.

It is my belief that we have a responsibility, an obligation to life, to ourselves, to the love that is our essence, to nurture it in ourselves and in every child we are graced to be with, to give and receive the gift of unconditional love. And when we sever or strain that sacred connection the child seeks and needs, it behooves us to mend it quickly and heal it.

Martin Luther King, Jr. expressed the belief that "unarmed truth and unconditional love will have the final word in reality." It is my faith that deeply we all concur in that belief. We hope that it may be true. Our part in realizing that hope must be to enjoin our attention and our lives to learning the art of loving. Humbly recognizing that we all have a lot to learn. And in that learning children are our best instructors, in the unbroken flow of their love, in their need, and in the challenges they will present to our loving.

Perhaps I should point out that this love is not that which monopolizes most of our cultural attitudes, our art, our thinking: it is not about desire, sex, intimacy, romance, marriage, the stuff of popular novels, music, movies – and advertising. The love of a child is greater than that. It is about closeness, identity, compassion and ever expanding consciousness. About the universal joy of connection.

Can you imagine a society that is truly based on love? Imagine a government where the representatives and administrators always exhibit love for each other and for the people, an education system where teachers show love for all their students, hospitals where the entire staff exhibits only love for you the patient, business and industry all operating out of love for the workers and for the clients and customers. If that could be in our dreams and in the stories we tell our children, they might work out how to manifest it for themselves when they grow up.

Love and joy, the positive feelings we seek to nurture in our core, are present as potential in every human being at birth. What we think of as negative emotions, fear, anger, grief, and so on are not present. They are reactions to occurrences in our lives that may come to disturb the peace of our love and enjoyment. Without these interferences our love and joy would be constant and undisturbed. Of course there will always be occurrences of loss, threat, and frustration that will produce these negative feelings. That is natural, but we are endowed with natural reactions to recover from these as well, which I have mentioned in the chapter about discharge – the healing of them. Understanding that what we as adult guides can do is listen, allow and encourage this discharge fully as it emerges from the child, and then to kindly offer guidance to assist the understanding and reparation of the damage.

What is most useful then is the practice of our tool of Supportive Listening. When the child feels that her distress has been heard and appreciated, that she then has the ability and understanding to handle such incidents, and that she has in you a reliable ally that will be on her side, she is able to quickly recover learn and grow from the experience. When children express negative emotions such as fear, anger or grief, we may sometimes react poorly, in a way that is not helpful to the child. We don't like their feelings. We want them to go away. Sometimes we just deny the feelings: "Don't be afraid – there's nothing to be afraid of." But if we manage to get the child to stop the expression, what we have stopped is not the feeling, which will continue unexpressed. What we have stopped is the *healing* of the feeling caused by the upset.

So it doesn't help to try and distract the child from her feelings: "How would you like some cocoa and cookies?" But it also doesn't help to go overboard in the other direction and become upset with her – that only dramatizes and adds to her confusion. Having a child scream or weep bitterly, shake or stamp or have a tantrum disturbs us and we feel we want to do something to stop it or fix it. But the best thing to do is stay close, be calm and attentive, listening sympathetically, taking the expression seriously, ready to stay through all the discharge. Showing by your attitude that you care, touching his hand – holding him if he will allow it.

By your calm acceptance of the child's feelings the hurt will eventually diminish, and he will have learned that he was able to handle it. His thinking will quickly return and you can encourage it, not by offering a solution, but by asking "What do you think now?" Giving him the freedom to explore his options for further healing. Or perhaps he will just shift into play mode – or go to sleep – he has used a lot of energy in that discharge and needs to recharge.

It is so empowering that you didn't try to take care of the problem, nor did you try to avoid, ignore, slight, or contradict his feelings. That you stayed close, concerned but not upset, showing not only understanding but also confidence in the child. That love and closeness is the best thing in life and will stay with you both forever.

West – Direction of Spirit

The last direction in the wheel of the complete person is what some people call spirit or soul. By that I don't mean anything to do with religion, with theology or a creed. Those subjects interest me greatly, they were the province of my doctorate studies, but they are for another book (I have no lack of things on my mind to write about if my energy holds!).

Spirituality is something we may not tend to speak or think about often. Most of our attention is about what goes on close at hand – close in space and time. What goes on in ourselves, in our thoughts and sensations, our relationships, to what we are doing or dream to do, and also to our community and what is happening in the world at large. Sometimes we think back on our history and the world's history, sometimes we wonder about the future of what we know, about the lives of our children and grandchildren as they grow.

What I mean by spirit is what is beyond all that, of which we have no direct knowledge – at least as I define knowledge. In time – what was before this universe, and what may be its destiny. In space – about connection to what we do not know. Who are we? If the cosmos is one being, then how is it all connected? How does that connection affect how we think and feel about ourselves, about our loved ones, about the life and history of our planet, about consciousness, time, and death?

Most of us consider some of these kinds of concerns occasionally, but many do not. I think questions like these come naturally at times to children. If they grow up in a religion the answers may be provided which they may then accept for their lives. But also later they may reject those answers and search further, or perhaps decide there can be no adequate answers and get on without further inquiry. As children grow they may ask such questions, and that is a wonderful opportunity for further closeness. Another chance to listen and encourage the child to explore her own thinking. A family circle can get closer by taking some time together to listen to each other's spiritual thinking.

Sobonfu Somé says, "When indigenous people talk about spirit, they are basically referring to the life force in everything." I think perhaps that may be true, from my connections with indigenous people in many parts of the world. Indigenous people have a special understanding of life force. It is found in stones, in wind and water, we can feel it everywhere, and the stars speak to us in the same way. Spirit, as we understand it, helps us make the connection to everything, past, present, and future.

Community is important to us, in order to be fully ourselves, that is to be a full human being. And it is spirit that guides us, guides the community, that connects us. It is important for all of us, elders, men, and women and children, to come together sometimes and connect in the spirit of our community.

We sense that a child when it is born is coming from a deep connection with spirit as it has been deeply connected to the mother in the womb. If we are paying good attention to the child growing, we may hear pure and wonderful insights of spirit that she has understood. Children often have refreshed and renewed my consciousness of spirit in this way. So I pay attention.

The Great Separation

The Circle Way recognizes that humanity is suffering today from disconnection, a Great Separation from basic needs and values of humanity, suffering from the isolation patterns of our societies. There are three major separations affecting us all. We are suffering from our separation from Mother Nature, from the Earth and all other life, both plant and animal. Secondly, we are all suffering from our isolation and separation from each other. We have lost our tribes, our communities, even the closeness of our families. And finally we are separated from our very selves. We do not know who or what we are, our real nature, our spirits, our very souls are hidden in the identifications we are given and taught by our societies – that we are only consumers, customers, producers, taxpayers, voters, numbers identified in polls, victims of history as others write it. When I begin to assert to people the truth of their goodness and innocence, of their lovability and their compassion, of their caring and helpfulness, of their playfulness and creativity, of their longing for and deserving of any kindness, appreciation and understanding, they usually laugh or weep to hear this great and immensely vital truth.

As human beings we have a number of needs, not only for food and exercise and rest and meaningful occupation. We all need to be heard. And beyond that we also need to be understood. And beyond that we need to be accepted by others. And beyond that we need to be appreciated, to feel valued by our fellow human beings. And we need the security and warmth of knowing we belong. Belong to the Earth and perhaps some particular part of it, belong to the community, the clan and family where we live, and that every part of ourselves is accepted and valued by our selves.

Reconnecting

In The Circle Way we are not seeking to copy cultures of other times or places in our ways of relating and of caring for children. We look to other cultures to see what may work well (or ill), but we seek to create our own ways of relating to each other, to children, to the environment, to life, to our sense of evolution and our sense of rightness, of beauty in the universe. We seek to understand and learn from traditions without feeling bound to any. We want to base our relations and actions on who we are today and what we have learned from all our studies and experiences. Then it is interesting and fitting for us to create our own myths and stories, our own ceremonies and celebrations based on our highest aspirations.

There is no one right way. We do not seek perfection. But we are continually striving to discover what is better. We are all different, but we have many common needs, and we have the ability to learn and work together for ways that work better for all.

The Circle Way is a way arising from us to make our lives better by coming together and listening to each other. It recognizes that people's needs may be different, but that all of us need sometimes to be close to other people and sometimes to be apart from people. There is no single best ratio of that for everyone, but all of us need sometimes to be heard and to listen to others.

So The Circle Way is concerned with connection, and it is concerned with learning the art of listening as part of the art of loving. In our larger communities and gatherings we come together in small circles, small enough that in the allotted time everyone can be listened to well. Sometimes these circles can be as small as two people, or three or four. If a circle has more than ten we may want to consider splitting into two circles so that everyone can be fully heard.

We organize the structure in a way that each person may have an equal amount of time to share both feelings and ideas, and each person may choose someone to act as an active primary listener who is able to support and encourage the exploration of his feelings and ideas. In that way the person need not be confused by many people interjecting help, so the rest of the circle will only listen passively. Other people's thoughts about what was expressed can be shared in review later. And each small group can later share the matters from the smaller circles that may be of importance and interest to the larger circle through a designated representative.

One of the principle reasons that people feel powerless and frustrated is that they are not heard. We need to make our decisions together, from groups small enough that each voice is attended to. Now the political and economic organizations are too big, the numbers of people too great. Their feelings and ideas are available to decision makers only through opinion polls and periodic voting, not through face-to-face working through differences with respect and understanding.

If we could remind ourselves continually that children are not different from us, that they are people whose feelings and ideas are important to them, who feel powerless and hopeless when they are not listened to seriously with respect, then we may have more understanding of them, be a greater help to them in finding the skills and confidence to deal with the world, and create more closeness and trust. While needing time to themselves, unless they are resolved to be hermits, people need other people.

We need to be listened to and understood, we need to feel wanted and accepted, we need a group that knows and appreciates us where we know we belong. We are all interesting and often delightfully different, but we share many common feelings and needs. In The Circle Way we are all important and deserving of attention and, yes, celebration, and we can choose to give and receive these with each other, and

TOGETHER THERE IS NOTHING WE CANNOT DO.

Chapter Eleven
Parents Liberation

"The power of the world works in circles."

–Black Elk

What all of us, adults and children, parents and grandparents, educators, politicians, thinkers and communicators need to recognize is that in our age of great movements to remove persecution and liberate oppressed groups, the most important of groups has been ignored: parents.

Parents perform the most important of all work in this world, demanding exhausting, full-time work. And for that they receive almost no support, honor, praise or encouragement and no pay. Little credit do they get for their children's achievements but all the blame for their transgressions.

Parents know this but feel hopeless to change society's attitude. Grandparents knew it but have forgotten. Educators, political leaders, and thinkers have little incentive to look at this obvious oppression.

Parents Liberation

Parents Liberation. When I mention this in lectures I get giggles and then sighs from the parents. It is a concept so little considered that it seems a funny fantasy. The oppressed people, we parents, have not really thought about it much. When we do, we recognize the oppression is real, parents are isolated, made to feel inadequate and guilty, overtired, and with little understanding or support from anyone, working for the future of all humanity.

Okay, let's think about it now. What will it take for real change? What will it take to become a real movement? Think about the other liberation movements. The destruction of the slave culture in America and the recognition of full equal human status for slaves was a long time coming, people writing and gathering to communicate, and even after the legal conclusion more than a century of liberation work was needed and the battle against racism and bigotry still goes on.

Similarly it took many decades of demonstrations and activism for women to be able to vote – a victory that has still to occur in some parts of the world today – and even now women do not receive equal pay. Sexism is alive and well in the civilized world.

The liberation movements began when people began to recognize their own oppression and to raise their voices against it. In other words when the oppressed people began to listen to each other and to recognize their oppression. But they would have gained no ground unless others outside the oppressed group also listened and understood the oppression and joined together to defeat it. Only when free people began to confront slavery could it be eradicated. Only when men joined with their sisters could they attain suffrage and political equality. And now in a relatively brief period the prejudices of centuries are quickly falling. Politicians no longer dare to speak disparagingly of other races, religions, or ethnic groups. Now public institutions must make facilities available for the handicapped. The idea that people of the same sex should be allowed to marry and love unashamed is suddenly spreading and being welcomed through America.

Parents! It's our turn! We are overdue. Be silent no more. Speak up! Gather together! Listen to each other. Begin making circles of parents. Call out for allies and build a worldwide movement!

It takes a village to raise a child, and it takes a community to be heard and begin to effect change. When women began to speak up and listen to one another, they became a community and the voices of their community began to resonate, attracting both other women and caring men as allies.

At this time there are many groups of parents who come together to help one another and seek support from local town, city, and state governments. More than mere isolated groups are needed. A massive world movement is called for. I look forward to more women, more mothers and fathers taking this larger view of parent liberation. Speaking out. Writing articles, pamphlets and books. The sanity and justice of the world and the future of the Earth and our children are at stake.

That village that can support the care of our children does not yet exist in the First World. So we must create it. Yes, we. While I live I see this as this biggest initial step toward all our liberation, towards a more human society and a greater scope for the creativity of our children. And I am prepared to support and facilitate that movement in any way I can.

If you are a parent I want you to talk about this with other parents, and with non-parent allies. If you are not a parent, find a parent to talk with about all this. If you feel unsure of how to do that, I suggest you try the tools you have read about here, "The Circle Way", "Play Days", "Special Time", and the tool I call "Supportive Listening", or co-counseling as it is known to the Re-evaluation Counseling community that developed it. Because that method allows the greatest expression of your feelings and the resultant clearest appraisal and use of your creative thinking. "None of us is as smart as all of us."

Then reach out to other parents and keep expanding your circle, listening, feeling, discharging, thinking together regularly. Building your village. If you are already a co-counselor or have an opportunity to learn and join a Re-evaluation Counseling area – you will find ready parents there whom you can reach out to and form a parents support group. If there are already parents groups in your area, seek them out. Parents are a joy to be with, to share our trials, our goofs, our bewilderment – we are all in the same boat – it's crazy, desperate, comical, and none can appreciate it so well as us.

Once you have a circle of parents that meet regularly you can brainstorm on ways to use it to support each other in parenting. One thing I would strongly recommend is that you all come together for a "play day." Play days are fun for all and bring us closer to each other and the children. See if you can manage it at least once a month to start.

In our community here in New Hampshire play day was the one mandatory event we planned at the start of every month. Everyone had to clear their schedules for it because we all agreed that it was the most important event for both the children and the adults. We all went to Otter Lake Park, or to a beach at the seashore, and we had a picnic, and we played. We took turns playing with different groups, using the ways discussed in Chapter Four. We generally managed to have one adult for each child and another group of adults who might share memories and feelings about their own childhoods and how it was to play then. After an hour or so the ones sharing memories might go to play with the children and the ones who had been playing make circles to share the feelings that were coming up about their own childhoods. Then there were also times when children played with each other and adults played together. At the end of the day we were all exhausted, happy, and close.

Both of those could get so popular with your circle that others hearing of it would want to join. Maybe you will want to have them once a week instead of once a month. Both the giving and the receiving are pure fun! Maybe it will grow into many circles that might hold a joint Play Day gathering annually.

Recently there has started a movement to inspire pillow fights around the world for everybody, children and adults. Ellika and I attended an International Pillow Fight Day event in Cambridge Common. We found about 300 people gathered, bearing their pillows (as instructed without zippers or feathers), and at a signal all began happily bashing each other. There were college students, young adults and older men, children of all ages and their parents. I saw a couple of tots in strollers gaily swatting passers-by, and many photographers appeared snapping photos of us oldsters joining the fray. Much laughter and hilarity. I retired after what seemed like hours, and checked my watch to find it was only 30 minutes of cushioned mayhem.

An Invasion of Helpers

Another suggestion I would offer is what our co-counseling community has done sometimes, to select a family and organize a helpers raid on it. The helpers arrive and several give attention to the children and play with them while others do the dishes, mop up the floor, take out the garbage, cook the dinner, and still others give attention to the parents with Supportive Listening. Pick a family every month and have a blast!

Still another idea, when your parent circle starts to get close and to know each other, might be sometimes to split up into the mamas and the papas. The women together might share their feelings about the work and play of mothering and how it could be made better, including what help they would like to have. The fathers meeting could also share feelings of what it's like for them to play with the children and lose, letting the young people feel powerful, and what problems might arise for them and what help they could use – as well as what the parents might do to think and be close and offer help to each other. Sometimes the children could be invited to come to the parent's circle to give feedback and make suggestions.

The Making of Schools

One thing which many parents have done is to join with other parents to create a school. In the late 1960s I had a woman partner in San Francisco who had a daughter, and when she approached school age we began searching for an appropriate school. There existed then two very fine free or alternative schools, small and lovingly designed by and for parents, children, and congenial progressive teachers. One, a pre-school attached to a church, was called the Hearth School, and the other for elementary years was called The Shire School. For each there was a considerable waiting list of parents who longed for such a school for their children. The waiting list decided to contact each other and discuss making a new school of our own.

We parents met often all summer long, and by September we

had our act together enough so that we had a number of committed parents prepared to contribute as teachers and organizers, and a group of teacher students from San Francisco State College and other childless volunteers eager to step in and help develop our grand experiment. We rented a storefront and began our very first school. In a salute to our predecessor schools we called it Hearth-Shire.

It was a "free school", inspired by A. S. Neill's Summerhill, and charging no tuition. People freely donated whatever they could afford, to pay the rent and take care of expenses, and donated books and materials. Many of the people involved were living communally in various houses and the whole school felt like a community – the embryo of the village

I went in every day. Other parents went in when they could fit it in their schedules. A few parents had no time to give, but were able to give money instead. Everyone offered their skills in crafts or knowledge of interesting subjects. My favored contribution was to take a class every day on a field trip in the city, to museums, libraries, the aquarium, the zoo, the chocolate factory, the Mission, Golden Gate Park, Twin Peaks, ferry trips to Alcatraz or Angel Island, and exploring Marin County. It was a time of student demonstrations, against the war and for free speech, and the whole school would make placards and banners and parade proudly their sentiments before the barricades when we were assured that all would be peaceful. They really enjoyed that and learned a lot.

Hearth-Shire School, which had based its incorporation papers on those of the Hearth School, is no more, but it had a long and exciting history. There were always two factions, one which was devoted to life in that great city, its cultural, educational and political fullness, and one which longed for the peace and natural beauty of the California landscapes. On a camping trip in 1971 they were offered land and a group of the country faction split off to go to Humboldt County. When I returned to the Bay Area in the 70s I found Hearth-Shire still active in San Francisco with a country branch up north. Both groups ceased their functioning later but many who were involved, under the designation The Hearth School, which they had devolved to, still have been gathering annually at summer solstice and hold workshops on learning crafts, wilderness skills, creating ceremonies, and celebrate those memories.

The Palo Alto School

From the co-counseling community in that area a consistent and effective support for parents was developing, and in the fall of 1973 parents of young children began meeting bi-weekly to learn to counsel their children and to understand better how to see them as fully functioning human beings. The meetings were led by Tim Jackins, the Area Reference Person for Re-evaluation Counseling there, and out of them grew the Palo Alto RC School. In 1975 Patty Wipfler took leadership of the parents' group, and she and Sara Wordsmith became co-directors of the school which began to operate in September of that year. A description and monthly journal of that first year of the school is presented in the pamphlet *Permit Their Flourishing* (see bibliography) which anyone thinking of bringing parents together to form a school would do extremely well to study.

In Philadelphia, Chuck Esser, who is the Re-evaluation Counseling International Community Reference Person for Family Work, and who helped us in the early stages of my own learning of this work when our children were still small many years ago, has created a school similar to the Palo Alto model and has introduced the concepts into the city high schools.

Since no liberation movement succeeds without people joining from outside the oppression, we are going to need to bring in non-parent allies. You might hold events to which non-parents are warmly invited. You will want them for Play Days to be sure of two adults per young person. You can tell the non-parents that playing with children is the most fun and very rewarding. One gets to hang out with lively young people who have some very interesting perspectives on the world and are very happy to be with you and want to be friends. And you will learn a lot about yourself. About your childhood memories and influences that still affect you. It's a chance to get closer to people of different ages and to learn more of the art of Supportive Listening. You might manage to get some young people who have enjoyed Special Time and Play Days to talk about what they like about them.

When you have had regular Special Time and Play Days with young people you will be in a position to tell potential allies that spending time with children has filled your life with a lot more joy and fun.

Spending Special Time playing with children that are not your own gives you the opportunity to make a big impact on their whole lives. By choosing to spend time with them you can contradict all the belittling and demeaning and even humiliating experiences they are likely to have in schools and playgrounds, in offices and stores, in hospitals – even at home, everywhere in our society. You can give them a better understanding of reality – of how good, how smart, how interesting, how caring, and how important they are. How important they are to you, and how important they are to the world.

And you will be a V.I.P. – a very important person in their lives. For only a short period, a few minutes, a few hours, an afternoon, you can provide a picture of who that child is and how she can make a difference in this world that she will never forget.

When I was a boy, in the summers of my six through eight years, there was a college boy who my grandmother engaged to teach me to swim and sail. He taught me much more. He told me stories that he made up based on my interests and love of adventure, and he taught me how to draw as he illustrated his stories, encouraging and advancing my dreams of storytelling, art, and adventure. When I was forty I organized a clean-up in the streets of San Francisco, and my call for volunteers resulted in a response from Fred Comee, whom I had not heard of in over thirty years, now a vice-president of US Steel, who took me sailing on the bay in his sloop. He had never forgotten the little boy he loved and made up stories for, and I had never forgotten Fred, who gave my childhood a wider and better picture of the world and its possibilities than anyone else.

That is a gift that non-parents and parents of children who have grown up can bring to any child and receive the distinct joy of connecting deeply to children without all the other many responsibilities of parents. With only the responsibility of giving your attention, your caring, and your best thinking to them.

Parents need each other's support in the face of the disapproval and lack of understanding of so many whose beliefs were formed by the traditions of the civilizations that grew in Europe and Asia during the past ten thousand years. Traditions often can become so ingrained in cultures that they are unquestioned and seem to their inheritors the only right way to behave.

Take heart. We live in a very different world from the one I grew up in, where women's place was in the home and they were subordinate everywhere to male dominance, where in the southern United States every facility was delineated with signs for "white" or "colored" and African Americans faced the threat of violence in every quarter of the US, where also those who felt the "love that could not be spoken" were closeted in terror of humiliation, often fearful for their very lives. There is more understanding of human rights and more consciousness of their violations worldwide. But still the oppressive situation for parents remains, with little mention or honor except on those commercial occasions called Mother's Day and Father's Day geared only to sell cards and gifts.

Shall we change this? We can, you know.

In Europe the questioning of those traditions began to reach people's minds through novels of the eighteenth and nineteenth centuries, especially Dickens, and with child-focused thinkers in the middle of the twentieth century, so that now our library shelves are filled with books of more enlightened instruction, there are classes and workshops for parents, and family therapy available, as well as homeschooling and alternative schools, all derived from a full new respect for young people.

In that atmosphere the parenting circles you may form will be welcome. The ways that you as a group choose to relate to other young people, to give them freedom of choice in determining their paths and their studies, to listen to them and encourage their voices, and to be open to work on your own limitations and even learn from young people – these may not be seen as welcome or desirable to many still adhering to the old traditional concepts. But the parents and the children will benefit.

The older generations may see these new ways as criticism of them, and people in education and other professions that deal with children will often want to prevent any alteration of the status quo. It will be important for our new parenting circles to be confident and compassionate, to listen to all objections with understanding, and gently explain the reasons and note the positive results of this new way of relating to young people, the understanding of them as full and complete human beings, needing only our love and appreciation and gentle guidance – the guidance not of a subordinate but of a beloved friend, a teacher who is still learning and loves unconditionally.

The best way to introduce others to this way is to create occasions where they may observe your interactions with young people. They may be disturbed by the way in which you try to connect and not control. They may not ever have encountered this, and it may be strange to them. If they confront you about it you can say you are exploring different ways with them, trying things out, seeing what works, and what you are doing seems to be working well so far. If they then want to tell you why you are wrong, you can listen with interest and thank them for their input and say you will think about it. But you know from your own life that what will work best is what the young people will wish for themselves. As you would have when you were a child.

The parenting circles ought to be fun. Life is supposed to be fun. If it's not fun who would want to commit to it and help it to grow? Maybe there could be a Director of Fun, who thinks of light and lively things to do at each gathering, games, dances, songs, talent shows. There could be many leadership opportunities for folks, roles that could rotate periodically. One to set the agenda for the circle, another could be time-keeper. One might be the caller who gets in touch with folks to see who is coming and who needs help to come and calls people later who missed the circle to tell them what happened and say they were missed and do they need help.

Another role could be the beauty and order of the meeting place – before and after the circle, providing tissues to cry into, seeing that there is a safe place for playing, maybe a quiet place for naps, some mats for roughhousing, games and toys (not too many), perhaps snacks. Another role might be a presenter of some subject, a talk on some aspect of parenting, a book report, and discussion in the circle or in small groups or dyads.

I hope that by the time you have read through to this chapter you have already at least tried out "Special Time." It may be a good idea to bring that up as a topic very early and often in your circle. Reports from people about their Special Time sessions with their children. What has been good in those sessions? What has been hard in them? Supporting and encouraging each other to provide a regular schedule of weekly Special Time for each parent with each of their children, so the young people can look forward to them and prepare what they would like to do in them, and so that the sessions may get deeper and closer and perhaps sometimes longer. What have you learned about your child from these sessions? Has she begun to open up more of her inner thoughts and feelings to you? Are you able to show your complete appreciation and enthusiasm in everything your child is doing and showing you?

There also could be a time to discuss and explore how non-parents and parents both benefit from making occasional Special Time dates with children not their own and for reports about any of those that have happened.

Family Workshops

Family workshops are a further and important event you might create for your parenting circle. Not right away, because you will all need to know each other and the material dealt with in this book quite well before you begin to plan your first workshop. But they are a wonderful support for your parenting community, for every family, every parent and child involved. So you will want to start thinking about it learning and discussing and planning from very early on.

I would recommend a study and discussion of this book and the others listed under co-counseling in the bibliography. Those of you who are or become members of a Re-evaluation Counseling community can attend their family workshops and experience how they work. You could also gain much understanding by participating in one of our Circle Way Camps. From your own circle's Play Days and from your sharing of Special Time experiences, you might be able to organize your own Family Workshop with the leadership of those from within the circle who have the most experience and understanding of how to direct a really good workshop. An excellent guide would be the booklet *Family Work,* and further information and inspiration can be gained from *How Parents Can Counsel Their Children,* by Tim Jackins, and *Listening Effectively to Children,* by Patty Wipfler, all available in English from Rational Island Publishers. (The last has also been translated into German by one of our Circle Way people.)

Now let's say you have a good circle growing and learning and supporting each other. How can you reach out further? How about the social networks on the Internet? Reaching out to other parents around the world. A good start right now for you would be the organization Hand-in-Hand Parenting which you may visit on the Internet at www.handinhandparenting.org. There you can communicate with people who have been working this way for many decades, where you can get materials, find classes, and a blog to connect with other parents, tell your story, ask questions. We would also be glad to connect with you at www.circleway.org where you can find articles, our schedule, a blog to share with us and others, and subscribe to our frequent articles. Other websites are also listed in the appendix of this book.

In your circle you can brainstorm other ways of reaching out. Events you could organize to raise consciousness. Give your group a name, a slogan and a logo, and write a manifesto, make it known. Give talks in schools and churches, libraries, have discussions and panels. Create social events, block parties, concerts. Show films. Organize political actions. Demonstrations. Street theater. Parades.

Perhaps organizing a county or state family fair that would have games and fun for the whole family and for adults and children separately, and provide a child care area operated by people in your circle where people could observe your relating to young people. Offering class and materials and information about parenting by connection instead of coercion, about Play Days and Special Time and Parents Circles, with circles and group discussions, singing, dancing, talent shows, and theater about Parents Liberation. It could become the hit event of your area annually, and delight the merchants (bringing tourists and money!).

Picture circles proliferating, camps and workshops and fairs everywhere, getting organized and networking throughout your country. Becoming a strong voice to influence public opinion, education, legislation, and the business world, and reaching out to other nations and cultures throughout the world.

One manual for bringing people together is my booklet *The Circle Way*, which is also available in the appendix of my book *Have You Lost Your Tribe?* For more information about parenting and parents liberation with the perspective of this book, see the bibliography of co-counseling resources in the appendix.

Society has always given the rules, warned and corrected us and not wanted people to get together, suspicious of thinking that might run counter to the rules. It wants the rules, not the parents, to decide what is best for our young people. A woman in Austria told me that her children's teacher was upset when she came to discuss her child's education and treatment in the school. The teacher's attitude was that it was none of the parents' business, and that the teachers were the professionals who knew best and the parents must follow the rules and do as they are told. That school, and all schools, need to hear from a strong circle of concerned parents.

We really need the circle. It's what made us human and what can keep us human, thinking flexibly with open minds to each other. We need to put out what we think and be heard and considered and to listen to what others think. We have learned from our history and from our children, and we can learn from each other.

Support for Parents

On the subject of how to create community support for parents, I bring to your attention the values of the First Nation communities of North America. This I derived from listening to native elders for so many years speaking about the values of their old traditional community ways and also to many parents and grandparents who spoke of the traditional family ways in which they had been themselves raised. In the closely interwoven tribal circles of the past all the adults felt a family connection to all the children. Every baby that was born was a source of celebration and pride to all, and was assured of that sense of belonging and being cared about all their lives as children, adults, and beloved elders.

In these circumstances the mothers and fathers, who were not alone and isolated in the care of the children as parents are today, had a much easier time of it. The clans also instructed the children, and clan mothers, clan uncles or aunties were on hand to guide and help the children to be honored and loved members of the community. The familiar axiom "it takes a village to raise a child" is understandable in this context.

We are a long way from those values in our society today. Extended families living in proximity and supporting each other are a rarity, there is a less than fifty percent chance that a nuclear family will remain intact for the raising of their children to adulthood, and there is little sense of community anywhere. How then could we return to the human values in which parents are integrated and supported by a caring community?

This is the question we are undertaking to address in our camps and family workshops, using such tools as "Supportive Listening," "Play time," "Special Time," community problem solving, celebration and ceremony and others you have learned about in this book. The overall term by which we refer to all of this is The Circle Way. Using The Circle Way in our camps and workshops we are bringing people together, contradicting the isolation and competitiveness of society to experience the conscious creation of a truly human community in which all are supported and cared for and valued and in which the joy of working and playing and creating together is embraced by a sense of belonging.

This is the goal we will broach in the final chapter, how to begin here and now to get parents together to support each other, to create that "village" for raising our children together, to begin to live in The Circle Way.

I have a large button on my hat with my favorite saying:

NONE OF US IS AS SMART AS ALL OF US.

Chapter Twelve
The Village

"It takes a child to raise a village."

—Manitonquat

I had three aims in writing this book. First of all to let more people know about the wonderful work being done on our relationships to children for the past forty years by many people in the international Re-evaluation Counseling community, inspired greatly by Tim Jackins and Patty Wipfler, whose writings are listed in the appendix. This work is the basis of much of the family workshops and camps my wife and I present in eleven countries at this writing.

My second aim, the focus of the previous chapter, is to promote and support the consciousness of Parent Liberation.

I hope you found those eleven chapters helpful in your caring for children. If you did I am satisfied this book did what I wanted. But my third aim for this book is the one in my secret heart and the one that makes this book unique.

The third aim is the subject of this last chapter. The ultimate aim. To encourage thinking about and developing that village which it takes to raise a child. The previous chapter suggests the beginnings of such a village in bringing parents together to listen and share and support each other. This chapter indicates how to take this village concept further to a community of people who tie their destinies to one another, to the children, and to the land, ecologically, culturally and spiritually.

The culture we have evolved, whose basis is material wealth and the concentration of it in the hands of a very few at the expense of billions of people who have not the means for adequate clothing and shelter, nutritious food, medicine and medical attention to say nothing of education, that culture with its wealth secures more wealth and maintains its control assuring that no significant change can affect that control. Every part of society is dominated by the oppression of profit as its motive: education, medicine, mental health, agriculture, workers, middle class, elders, every oppressed group, including women, and especially children. It is an inhumane society world-wide, not fit for human beings, and a hostile one for children.

We Need the Children

We need the children to center our lives on what is important to us, not on the struggles for material gain and show of wealth or the latest gadgets, not for prestige or position, not on all our distractions from those struggles, but for the deep joys of friendship and fun, playing and connecting with our children, as well as our elders and neighbor, in interesting and worthwhile enterprises benefiting all life on Earth. Children know and remind us that life can be fun, that work can be play.

So, playfully but seriously – it takes a child to raise a village. The central force in the lives of parents (and central to the future of humanity) are their children. The older traditions of North America teach us that we must concern ourselves not only with the lives of our children and grandchildren, but also of all the unborn generations that come after us.

It is children that can bring our greatest joy, and children that can bring us our greatest sorrow. It is children that can bring us our greatest headaches and our greatest fears for their safety. It is for our children that most of us worry during sleepless nights, work hard by day to provide a safe home, an education, and a good start in life. For their sake we make sacrifices and often limit our personal freedom and pleasure.

In our traditional village life the parents were not the only ones responsible for the care of the children. That responsibility, that obligation and that joy belonged to everyone, not only the parents and grandparents, also the uncles and aunts, and all the elders, to their clan mother and all the clan, to the whole village.

I have counseled so many people, mostly women but sometimes men too who said they had lost their childhoods because they had to take care of their younger siblings. Understandable, considering how overwhelmed parents of large families can be in our cultures where they get no support from other adults or from their society. Understandable but still wrong. No child should be put in that position and have to bear that responsibility for her siblings.

However, in our old traditional tribal societies the older children do watch out for the younger ones, do help and guide them in the ways of their people. They are not required to, they do it when and how they choose, but they are proud to transmit their knowledge, to help feed and clean and dress and keep the little ones from harm. That is not a responsibility they are asked to take, but, like all human beings, they enjoy being helpful and demonstrating their abilities, leadership, and caring, and of course are not blamed for neglect or mistakes. Caring for children is a joy all the community shares.

The prospect of children being cared for by a whole community, people who are closely connected to each other and devoted to all the children, working and playing together, listening to each other, sharing thoughts, values, feelings and celebrating together – this vision clarifies and contradicts the oppression of isolation and separation in which all of us, parents and non-parents alike, now struggle alone.

And when we consider that in the prehistory of all cultures it was the community, the tribe, the village that best supported the caring of young human beings and their parents, we well may long for that community village again. If our children are central to our existence, it might urge us to consider if and how we may construct such a village in our lifetime.

We want to be connected, we want to help each other, know each other better, love each other and play together as well as work together, to make life more wonderful for each other. We want a village of people whose voices we hear, whose eyes we see, whose hearts we know. Where there are cities we want them made of villages – integral communities of people who know and care for each other. Every apartment house could be a village, every floor could be a clan.

If that is possible and we are able to manifest it, that will be only one more reason to rejoice and to celebrate our children. We adults are separate, and longing for closeness and support even as we despair of finding them. Building a village for children will also fulfill our own needs.

All is Relationship

My elders taught that relationship is everything. Everything is related to everything in Creation, and all relationships are sacred. Not just our relationship to our children and our parents, our relationship with each person, every animal and plant, with the whole community of Earth, with the land and all it sustains. In reverence for all relationships we give our children the great joy of connection and friendship with all around us in every moment of life.

We human beings have evolved to the point where we can think about our evolution and direct it to our advantage, to enhance the human qualities we admire and eliminate those that hamper them. To enhance joy in our lives, joy in love, in beauty, in creativity, in discovering and learning, and eliminate hurting each other and our environment. We can imagine different environments that are beautiful and healthy, including different social environments, and changing them will change us. This will especially affect our children who are more flexible, more playful, more imaginative, more vulnerable than we adults. They are even more dependent on love than we, with less defenses, more open to joy and laughter and closeness.

We can help direct our evolution towards greater health, beauty, love, and joy for our descendants.

All of this is why I want to create a new environment now. A village where we increase our closeness, our joy and love, our creativity and fun, and change each other – with the help of our children as our guides.

> "It is not true that evil, destructiveness, and perversion inevitably form part of human existence... But it is true that we are daily producing more evil... When one day the ignorance arising from childhood repression is eliminated and humanity has awakened, an end can be put to this production of evil... something will change in the very next generation if we cease to expose our children to the abuse known as discipline and child rearing."
>
> –Alice Miller

There are already thousands of communities devoted to living sustainably, to living in harmony and peace – ecovillages, they call them, all over the world. Most of them still struggle in their relationships with each other and their children, having carried with them the separation and lack of trust of thousands of years of civilization. Eliminating that is our task. This book has suggested to me as I am writing it that if we decide to treat each other as we wish to treat our children we will also be changing ourselves.

That is something we can do in a consciously created community that cares for its own while maintaining good relations with the old society beyond. Such communities, being more attractive and attentive to our real needs of being heard, understood, accepted, appreciated and belonging, would proliferate and by networking and supporting each other eventually supplant the society of fear, domination and conflict.

The Village! Can you imagine it?

Can you imagine a culture of cooperation and mutual caring and support? Can you imagine living among people who work together for the good of all? Not just for the human community, but for the animal and plant life – the whole community of the Earth. Can you imagine living with people who really listen to each other and trust each other and love each other's children? People who can be sure of the food all their children eat, that it is free of unhealthy chemical additives and genetic modification, because they produce it themselves.

Many of you reading these thoughts will no doubt think this is just the stuff of utopian dreams – pie in the sky. You need to know this is already going on, all over the world, although you rarely hear of it. There are such communities on every continent, in North and South America, in Europe, Africa, Asia, Australia as well as New Zealand and other island nations. You can find out more about them in my last book *Have You Lost Your Tribe?* There you can also read about the community we created in New Hampshire beginning in 1978, its twenty-year history and what we learned. It was a wonderful experience, initiated by our desire to make a better life for our children. It wasn't perfect, of course. But we learned from our mistakes – it was better than any of us had when we were growing up. And our children thrived on it.

Since then I have sat in many circles, lived in many communities, helped to create communities and to support many others. You really have no idea how much is going on right now around our world – new communities, co-housing groups, ecovillages, transition towns cooperating to live sustainably. I don't even know the extent of all that at this time, but I continue to meet representatives from new communal action groups in all the conferences I attend.

And I continue to visit and participate in many activities of communities. I am an honorary member at large of the ZEGG community; I have been very close to my friends at the Tamera community since long before they started that in Portugal; there are three communities in Austria now who are using our Circle Way to organize and build trust and intimacy; Elena's parents group is beginning an urban project now in Bologna and are seeking land to begin their child-centered community; there is a network of over 30 communities in Italy who are interested in learning The Circle Way; and since we have introduced The Circle Way at a workshop in Ireland a year go and again at a camp in Cork last May, that group has been meeting every month, has begun to acquire land and to move together with the goal of creating a Circle Way Village.

It is evident there is a new culture being born in these communities, which extends to the whole movement of worker cooperatives, farm cooperatives, consumer cooperatives, alternative free schools, and other non-commercial coalitions of people binding together to realize common goals.

There are many consciously designed and constructed communities everywhere in the world today. Our first child was born in one: The Farm, in Tennessee. I have many good friends who live in others in the US, Denmark, Norway, Finland, Germany, Austria, Italy, Portugal, and I have met many more from distant lands around the world. More than you would imagine, all different. So many you would take a long time to visit them all. There is a spiritual city still growing in India, and an anarchist one in Copenhagen (where my wife Ellika has had a home since 1979). Most of these were founded in the 1970s and are still evolving. You can discover more of them through the Global Ecovillage Network on your continent – there are separate GEN networks for mutual support in the Americas, in Europe, in Africa, Asia, and in the Pacific.

When we study the history of human cultures one thing can be said of them all. They change. Change is inevitable. However we live today it is not how our grandparents lived and it is not how our grandchildren will live. Predicting how it will change is an entertaining but unreliable activity. Still, we have a choice, whether to just live through, observe and record the changes, or to take an active part in creating change.

The model that began my thinking more than forty years ago about how this culture regards and treats its children, is that of the traditional native communities of North America. Traveling widely throughout the continent in the 1960s and 70s in order to discover the wisdom of my own heritage, I saw the remnants of the old ways where communities had been further removed from the genocidal path of European colonialism and had managed to retain much of the old ways of caring for their young. As I traveled, and also when I settled for a while in the 70s with the Akwesasne Mohawks, I spoke to parents of young and older children about their ideas and practices in child rearing.

I found that children in traditional native communities were respected and, in general, trusted. They were not lectured to and were not ever punished. That was so different from the dominant culture that I was intrigued. So I spent time when I could with the children. They were not closely monitored by adults and were given much freedom in their movements and activities, but grandparents, clan uncles and aunties did watch out over the young for their safety, and corrected them gently but firmly when they felt it necessary. The older children gave information, which was readily accepted by the younger ones who looked to them as models.

Being forced by law to attend the government schools, they naturally hated it, as do most young people. But free of the classroom and free to choose what interested them, they were naturally quick learners. They called all the elders grandfather or grandmother, and they called all the generation of their parents uncle or auntie, so for an outsider it would be at first difficult to distinguish among the families. They were full of energy and high spirits, ran together in groups, laughed a great deal, and arranged games easily and quickly with each other. They called me grandfather and were very interested in me as someone from outside their world. They asked many questions about my life, and when they heard I was a storyteller demanded often from me the tales of my people.

Where native communities had not been torn apart by relocation, unemployment and poverty, alcohol and drugs, and had been able to retain a considerable autonomy, the children could be trusted to maintain their respect for adults because respect was what they received and what they knew. (See appendix: "Joyous Childraising".)

Since the way Emmy and I wanted to treat our children with complete respect ran counter to what we saw in the world around us, including in many consciously created communities and spiritual communities we had visited, and that there was only one other person in my own nation who was ready to try and create and live in a traditional native village circle, we decided to build our own community. We decided to try and find others who would be willing to be completely respectful of the young people and to guide them by connection rather than coercion. In spite of the fact that none of us had grown up in such an atmosphere we managed to achieve that most important aim, by agreeing to listen to the children and to each other.

That period of our lives is over. Our sons, who grew up and went to college while in that community, are now parents themselves and have traveled far – one at the moment with his wife and two sons lives in Guatemala, the other with his wife and daughter lives in Berlin, Germany. As I have told you before with unabashed admiration, they are each caring, thoughtful, exemplary fathers. (And husbands, as well, of course.)

The community we grew in New Hampshire, Mettanokit (meaning Our Mother Earth), was excellent but too small to be a real village, averaging about 15-25 adults plus children over its years. The Farm in the USA, ZEGG in Germany, and Tamera in Portugal, favorites of mine, have around 200. Christiania in Copenhagen, where we also have a home, has about 850, Damanhur in Italy has around 1,000, and Auroville in India about 2,300.

Changing the World

My book *Changing the World* is a vision of a Circle Way village that contains everything I could think of that would suit me personally in every aspect I care about. I thought of it as having around five hundred adults and young people, organized in smaller circles called clans, with an organic farm that could feed them all, a dairy farm, sheep for wool they could weave, fruit orchards, greenhouses, permaculture, alternative sustainable energy production from sun and wind, educational buildings for all ages, shops and cottage industries, a café, music school and concert hall, an art school and a gallery, a theater, an amphitheater, a peaceful woodland trail with pond for meditation, a library, a museum, their own bank, post office, and a hotel for tourists and visitors. You can read *Changing the World* on www.circleway.org, but here is an excerpt, where the guide is explaining about the children of the village:

> "Well, there's a lot to learn about children, more than we can get into today. We do have courses here and at the other villages, for parents and teachers and other allies to young people, and there's a lot of good literature on that too in our bookstore, some we published ourselves. What I can say is that we never allow anyone to mistreat anyone or destroy things people need. We stay very close to all our children and step in to help them when there's a need. We will restrain a child lovingly but forcefully, hold him or her in our arms, and let the child use up all that destructive energy screaming, fighting to get loose, shouting hate-filled curses, crying, all the while we stay calm and understanding and caring, until, when those feelings have been discharged and the child is exhausted, we can further assure the child that we really do understand and care about him and maybe even get him to talk about the problem and his feelings. We let him know that, just as we won't let him hurt anyone, we will never let anyone hurt him.
>
> "We will do this in a sincerely friendly way, lightly, and maybe with some humor and certainly playfulness. We will be sure to stay close, to give him special time to do things he likes. And we will try to see to it that other children understand his struggle and accept and help him. The acceptance of one's peers is the most powerful motivator in tribal society, another good reason we need to stay very close to each other."

The building on the other side of the playground is the school, with classrooms and workrooms for all ages. The very youngest, what we might call the pre-school and kindergarteners have a little fantasy house of their own, looking like a mixture of fairy tales from many lands. There are no classes today, Sunday. Some of the rooms have no furniture, only cushions or mattresses.

"From what we heard today, you folks don't hold to compulsory education. The kids don't have to go to school?"

"That's right. Education is something that goes on all the time, because children are born curious and love to learn. But then they get sent off to school to get learning stuffed down their throats until they learn to hate it. Human beings are intelligent and have lively minds before school begins its deadening processes and makes them stupid.

"Children here are never forced to go to school, but most of them want to and look forward to it every day."

"That must be some school! Not like the one I went to!"

"Well, you see, it's their school. They get to decide what to learn, what we will do there, and we get to figure out what resources we need to provide. We work it out together, as with everything in the Village. We have teachers who are excited to help them and transmit that excitement in learning to them. They want to show the children the wonders in Creation, to provoke their thinking. There were models for this, Summerhill in England, Sudbury Valley in Massachusetts, for instance. And we keep experimenting, working to improve on it, with the help of the students. The main thing is to have fun, to have school be a place where we play a lot and laugh a lot and it's safe for children to express their thinking and their feelings.

"Children want to come because that's where the other children are and where the action is. In the outside world school is boring: lectures, homework, tests, grades. Here school is never boring. It's when you are not in school when your friends are and you are trying to figure out what to do all alone that you might get bored and decide to go where the fun is."

"But how can you avoid big classrooms and regimentation?

Do you have so many teachers?"

"We have as many teachers as there are people – everyone is potentially a teacher. Of course we don't all do it in the school, but many of us do put in a few hours now and then to show the children a skill, tell stories, talk about life, take a group on a trip somewhere, organize a group project, or just play with them. And most of the young people are self-starters. They are very resourceful and they set themselves their own projects, maybe get others to join a group project of their own. If there's a teacher available and interested, great, but if not they will figure it out on their own – maybe check in with an adult advisor now and then.

"You understand that most of what society calls school is only warehousing, keeping young people off the streets while people go to work. Here parents like to bring their children to their work, just as our ancestors used to. You know, a person could, not having set foot in a classroom for eleven years, easily learn in less than a year all it would take to pass examinations and get a high school diploma.

"But what is important for a human being to learn? How to do things, how to create, that's easy to teach, but the most valuable thing to learn is how to value yourself and take care of yourself, how to be excited about living and learning, how to enjoy the company of people, how to love. Isn't that right? Our teachers really love young people, love interacting with their developing minds. In our school you can not only learn all the traditional academic subjects, but also take courses in relationships, in conflict resolution, in working for world peace, in social and economic justice, in the care of animals, plants, and the environment."

"And technology?"

"Oh yes! There's plenty of interest for that. But our young people are very concerned about how technology is used. They think about whether what they work on will really benefit the world. Weaponry does not interest them. There are other villages that really specialize in technology, and many other studies – oh, medicine and health, for instance. This village as you have perhaps heard is known for its music and fine and performing arts schools. The concert this afternoon is a string quartet of teachers playing some especially wonderful classics of the European tradition."

There is more detail in the book about the economy, ecology, education, sports, the residences grouped around community houses, sub-communities or clans, where people gather, each with the major appliances they share, washing machines, audio and video equipment, and workshops for home and machine work. Perhaps I will go back and fill in more detail later, add more about ceremony and spiritual communion, perhaps rewrite it as a novel so more people might read it.

So what about your village?

My point is that you can have your village. It really is doable. Been done. In many ways. It will take time and thought. But the ecovillages we have now took only a few years to get established and growing. Look, I am sure you and others like you could make a much better community and society than you now have, and with likeminded folks and enough determination you can build it exactly to your design. Probably it will come out differently than expected – that's how it goes. But that's okay too. It's a learning experience, and it's an adventure. The wonderful thing about the circle is how it finds its own direction, how it shows us what no one of us could have thought of, continually surprising us with its wisdom.

And if you feel as I do that modern society is a toxic environment for human beings, especially bad for raising healthy happy children, maybe you should really take this seriously – or do you have something more exciting planned for your life?

So what to do? Well, we do have the vote. We can vote in new people with new ideas. How's that working out for you, by the way? We can get involved and try to change this system from inside. A noble cause. I wish you luck.

Well, cultures change, and this one is changing. But so slowly. Am I impatient? Yeah, I guess – I am enjoying my 86th winter now and wonder how much more I will have a chance to participate in. I grew up in the 1930s and survived a very different world from this one. A lot of the changes have been for the better, for women and minorities especially. A lot of diseases have been cured, communication and transportation are faster. But by the news every day people seem to be getting crazier, and the environment is a disaster and perilous.

What are our options?

What options have we to change the poisonous system in which we all struggle? Whatever you are doing to make things better I support and admire. But I truly believe that the best option we the people have is just to walk away from the system entirely – which thousands are doing now. But millions will eventually need to do that to start any real movement for a total change for the seven billion people on planet Earth. We need now to become as fully independent of the dominating cultures as much and as fast as we possibly can. We need to not make enough income from those cultures to pay them taxes, we need not to be dependent on them for food but grow all our own food and make what we need for ourselves out of what we can recycle rather than buy from supermarkets and department store chains. What we do buy we need to buy locally, preferably through people's co-ops, and make all the energy we can from renewable sources. We need to blow up our TVs and make our own entertainment, tell our own stories, make our own music and plays, art and literature, a complete culture of who we are, what we do and seek, our deepest dreams, deepest yearnings of our hearts, our humor and fun and playfulness with each other, to honor and be enriched by our elders and have fun and play with our children, and give them the experience that the joys of life are not about competition or winning or ownership or material stuff, gadgets, fashion, or wealth, but are found in our love, our connection and closeness to nature and other people and creatures.

There are thousands of communities around the world of people who have just contrived to leave their dominant malignant, polluting, destructive, manipulating, consumerist, corporate, industrial, insatiably greedy cultures. Those people have begun the process of re-connecting, listening to each other, to everyone equally, all genders, ages, and races, regardless of class or education. They have begun to make agreements together locally as to how to live and share together and support each other, and they are beginning now also to connect with other local communities in regional networks and with other regions around the world, to support and trade with each other.

Like many others, I have been engaged for many years in the process of empowering people to work together, to listen to each other, support each other, build trust and an environment where, by connection and cooperation, we can create whatever we dream of and agree we want. Our particular process we call The Circle Way, and what we are up to can be found at www.circleway.org. We have three communities in Europe now using our Circle Way process and two others in Ireland and Italy ready to acquire land and begin to build. But we are not alone – I meet with many representatives from other networks of communities around the world at gatherings where we inform and support each other. Most people do not yet know that this is going on, but as this grows we will start to conceive the shape of the new world our prophets and visionaries have told of, a world whose new culture is truly human, of, by, and fit for human beings.

As long as I live and can speak and write I will be encouraging people to walk away from the system and make their own, to help the communities that already exist to listen better to each other, to come closer to one another and bring ways to solve separateness and problems and more fun and compassion within them with the proven effective tools of our Circle Way and Supportive Listening, and to create new communities in The Circle Way and to support and create networking and closer connection among them and with all networks of alternative communities throughout the world.

"I want to begin to build a Circle Way Village which can be a model to the world... Who wants to come play with us and start to build a village and a world now?"
—Manitonquat

So – anybody with me? Are you stuck where you are, can't see how to get out? Maybe you say, why should I change? I'm doing all right, it's not perfect, but I worked hard to get where I am and you want me to what? To just walk away and start something different?

As a counselor listening to people for decades I am so aware of the continual stress that everyone is under in this culture, and I am aware of the essential isolation, the loneliness deep inside people. Of the effects of all that on everyone, and on our children.

Why do we put up with it? Because we are alone, because it seems we have no other choice. Still, you may dream of a better life, a better world. You know it could be better, something could be done – but what's the next step?

May I suggest The Circle Way? Of course you can't do it alone. But you are not alone – it feels like you are but that's just your isolation pattern – there are seven billion others stuck here with the status quo, and I am quite sure most of them don't like it the way it is. I'm pretty sure there are a lot of folks who feel the way I do, and a lot who feel the way you do – however that may be. Change starts with a circle. The circle starts with you and some other kindred soul. Let's say you and me. You have a dream. I listen to it and then tell you my dream. We keep listening to each other, active, supportive listening. We find others who are interested. The circle grows. We dream, we think, we plan, then when the time is ripe we build it. Together. It's an adventure. It's fun.

What is life if it's not fun? What is life but an adventure?

The Economic Issue

If you worry about the economics of it, let me just say that a group of people who pool their energy and resources can live on far less per person than each person living by themselves or in separate families can. Our community, all poor unpropertied folks, paid off a mortgage plus $50,000 in debts in 10 years. Such is the experience of every single consciously created community that exists today. And the difference between them and the ones that did not continue has only to do with the level of commitment. When people *want* to do a thing they find a way.

The hardest part, in my experience, is in learning to get along, to listen, to support and appreciate and celebrate each other. Using the tools of this book and of the other books listed in the bibliography will, I assure you, be more than sufficient. If you listen to each other, work together, and never give up.

Do you want to know what it takes to create and build a new community? I think, from what I've seen, all it takes is one person, one person totally committed, one person who is so dedicated that he or she will never give up. If he never gives up, that kind of dreamer attracts others, and because none of us is as smart as all of us, eventually, together they will find the way, will remove all the barriers and do it.

And once you have your circle, what it takes to keep it together is everyone's love and trust in each other and in the circle. The patterns of our old society will confuse some of us some of the time, but if we all care for the circle we can help each other, remind each other of the reality of our love and our joy and the importance of our adventure together – the importance to our children and to evolution.

Every relationship has a spirit, and the members of the relationship must care for and watch out for that spirit as they care for, watch out for themselves and for each other. There is a spirit to a good marriage that the partners love and care for as they love and care for each other, there is a spirit to a good and strong family that all members must care for and love, and of which they can be proud.

When you have a circle, give it a name, celebrate it, write songs for it, come closer, live closely, take care of your children together, play and have fun. And when your circle grows to a community, a village, make smaller circles, support groups, clans, that can stay in closer touch with each other daily, enhance their lives by listening, understanding, supporting, appreciating each other. And give those clans names, make clan songs and tell clan stories and celebrate together often and create ceremonies for the whole village. Circles that work best find excuses to get together often and have fun and connect deeply. Steady contact gives support and makes a difference in our lives. When it's not fun, look at it together and see what's off – life is supposed to be fun, our children remind us. What do we need to make it fun?

What will people need in your circle? Caring for each other we need to know. We need to learn how to ask "How can I help you make your life more wonderful?" And we all need to learn how to ask for help when we need it and not pretend we don't need it. We need each other – let's just agree to that. Let's remember that to agree to accept help is a great gift to the helper. We all need to be helpful.

If someone runs from the circle, understand that as distress – there is a hurt, there is a need – and don't let that person suffer alone. Go after her, it's only distress, after all. It's old stuff and not as important as being loved and heard right now. Show her you miss her and need her and love her, that there is a place only she can fill in your heart, that she is important to you and all the circle.

As babies we were born reaching out to others. When we were hurt by them we withdrew. We need to learn how to reach out again. We are all waiting for someone to reach out to us – who will be the first to do it?

People pretend they don't need anyone, but they are crying inside. When a baby cries we pick him up and hold him. We listen and try to understand. We have to go after those who run away – they are hurt and need to be held and listened to and understood, appreciated and accepted.

When we have circles regularly we can remind ourselves of this, get closer and listen to everyone. We can promise always to be there for each other – we are family. When a circle forms everyone should listen to everyone's life story to understand and know who they are.

We all want to belong, to belong to something that is healthy and nourishing and fun, that accepts and honors us. When we have ceremonies, when we have celebrations, when we have feasts, when we have play days together, we increase that spirit of community. Our community – where we feel safe and wanted and cared about.

Because everyone needs to be by themselves some times, in the woods, in their study, walking the hills, paddling a canoe on a quiet lake, we want our community to understand when we want alone time (but will check sometimes to be sure it's what we want and not an old isolation pattern).

And sometimes bring your community together with others to celebrate, make festivals, fairs, help with local needs beyond your community, join volunteer fire departments, emergency medical teams, help fund-raising campaigns, teach adult classes, offer child care opportunities, clean the highways, make recycling centers, create events to promote world peace.

I've done a lot with my life, with the nine-and-a-half decades I've been given so far. I don't know how many more years there will be, of course, but I'm going to use them connecting, playing, and writing. I've done a lot, and if there's time I might write a book about that too. But I'm still ready to start a new project and build with a circle of people our own idea of paradise. And take it as far as my time allows.

You want a village, a more human culture for you and your children? I'm listening. I know how to do it – or we do rather – and I know how to figure it out as we do it. What do we need? People. Resources (money). Land. Land large enough to invite people to gather and listen to each other, to learn how to do and teach supportive listening and spread the Circle Way. Enough land to feed us, for us to play and work together, enough for us to live as our ancestors lived, taking care of each other, of our children, of the plant and animal life, of our Mother the Earth.

What to do with cities? More than 50% of us live in cities now and soon it will be very much more. How can we get close to nature and to each other and to ourselves in the fast bustling anonymity of urban life? What I say to questions like that is, I don't know – I don't know, but I know that *we* do. There is nothing we cannot do when we put our minds together. We have just not universally recognized and understood this problem yet. It is huge but we cannot avoid it, and the time to begin to address it is now.

Perhaps it starts with meeting the neighbors, speaking our hearts and listing to each other. Then making circles – perhaps every floor of an apartment building becomes a clan and the whole building a village. It is the same process, reconnecting, listing to each other, getting closer to each other and figuring how to get closer to nature together, helping each other, building trust, creating, doing things together, caring for our children together, playing together, celebrating together – and networking with other communities, joining in larger entities, regions.

The communities I know that are sharing the work and resources and the care of the children are also living closer to the Earth, to the rhythms of nature and its lovely harmonies and beauty. They seek a natural healthy relation to their food through Permaculture and organic agriculture. What I am offering in The Circle Way is a Permaculture of the Heart – a process of regaining the natural flow of our love and compassion, of our closeness, playfulness and creativity together.

It begins, for me, with discovering ourselves, our own human nature, through connecting and encouraging and celebrating each other, then building our dreams together and reclaiming some portion of our beloved Earth to care for and belong to as we also belong to our families and our communities. As Chief Seattle said, the Earth does not belong to us, we belong to the Earth. That is the heritage we must pass on to our children, not possession but love of the Earth and each other and a joy in all life. We belong to all that.

Right now, all over the world this very minute, babies are being born. They are all just the same. They reach out to those around them, ready to love and to learn, to laugh and create, to connect and help others. They are all about to be pressed, crunched, clipped, mashed into their cultures and most of them will lose the hope they came with and conform to what is expected of them.

Humankind has become disconnected. Disconnected from the Earth, from its place in the unfolding of the universe. We all have been disconnected, separated from our hearts, isolated from each other, disconnected from strangers, friends and lovers, from our children, from the elders, from our communities and from ourselves, from our real natures and from the rest of life in all its beauty.

We know it, we can feel and relate to that need to connect. But it is confusing, awkward, alien to us – we have been so isolated for so long that we are afraid to reach out. Still, we were not born that way. Every little newborn baby opens her eyes and looks for other eyes, fixes on the faces and the smiles, and reaches out tiny fingers to connect.

Let that be our guide through all the confusion. Let us try to look on the world with all the freshness and wonder of children. Unless we become like unto one of them, we will not enter the kingdom of Heaven, which has been within us all the time. When we attend to their laughter, their fun, their joy, their longing for touch and closeness and play, their need to be heard and understood and loved, we are attentive to the true human condition, to our evolution and our destiny. When we have made our world right and good for our children, then it will be right and good for us all.

To end, a thought, from Omar Khayyam, by way of Fitzgerald:

Ah love, could you and I with Fate conspire
To grasp that sorry scheme of things entire
Would we not shatter it to bits and remold it
Nearer to the heart's desire?

TOGETHER THERE IS NOTHING WE CANNOT DO.

Epilogue
The Story of Muckachuck

When Maushop, our first great teacher, magician, and protector, had made the Earth safe for human beings, after he had gotten rid of all the evil giants, monsters, and sorcerers, he decided to move on, since the people were becoming too dependent on him. At his farewell ceremony where he explained to the people that he was entrusting the care of the Earth and all the other creatures to them, someone told him there was one more magician he had never met, Muckachuck, the most powerful magician of all. So Maushop decided that before he left he should check up on this Muckachuck to be sure he would not be a danger to the people.

Maushop found the magician's lodge on a hill where the people had told him to go. There was smoke coming from the smoke hole, so Maushop called out:

"Muckachuck! Are you in there? This is Maushop here. I'd like to talk to you. Would you like to come out or do you want me to come in?"

From inside came an unintelligible high-pitched babbling. So Maushop called again,

"I could not understand that. Are you inviting me to come in, or are you coming out?"

Again a lot of squeaky nonsense sounds.

"I still didn't understand. If you don't come out, I will assume you are asking me to come in."

More babbling.

"All right then, I'm coming in."

Maushop had to stoop to come through the low little door, and when he stood up inside at first he could see nothing. Maybe this magician has made himself invisible, thought Maushop. That could be a problem. But then he looked down and saw a little baby sitting on the ground in the center of the lodge.

"Oho, you have changed yourself into a baby to fool me," laughed Maushop. "That's a good job, you really do look like a baby! Well, I do a lot of shape-shifting myself sometimes too. Let me show you."

And he turned himself into a mountain lion and roared in the baby's face to impress him. But the baby wasn't scared. He laughed, and hugged the lion. Maushop a bit put off by this, turned himself into a snake and hissed in the baby's face. But the baby laughed again and hugged the snake. Then Maushop became an eagle and flew at the baby who laughed gleefully and hugged the eagle.

Maushop thought, this magician is getting the better of me, what can I make him afraid of? So then he transformed himself into a fire making a circle of flames all around the baby and came closer and closer. The baby looked all around, upset, and began to sweat. Suddenly he let out a pitiful cry and began to shake and weep.

Seeing the baby so terrified, Maushop was sorry and became himself again.

"Oh, baby, don't cry, it's just me. See? Maushop. I didn't mean to scare you like that."

But the baby kept on crying, so Maushop gave him his medicine bag from around his neck to play with. The baby hugged the medicine bag, stopped crying, and laughed.

"Oho – Now you took my bag! Well, take it, Muckachuck, It's my give-away for this visit. Something to remember me by. I think you are a good fellow and not a problem for the people. You didn't hurt me and I didn't hurt you, and we had some fun, eh? We can call it even. So I think I'll slip away and just pretend I never came. I won't tell anyone if you don't."

And Maushop left. Some say he is out behind the rainbow and could come back if we got in trouble and couldn't handle it. Maybe that's wishful thinking, but Muckachuck is still with us. Muckachuck means "little fellow" and he is the spirit of children everywhere, the little babies, and the ones waiting to be born. We say that is the greatest power we have, our true magic, and we say that, even today, if you go into a room and there's only a baby there all by himself, laughing and babbling and gurgling all to himself with no reason, we say, "You see, he's singing his war song and remembering the time when he beat Maushop!"

Afterword from the Author

I hope this book may have been some help in your life, and that you will be of even greater help to the children in your life, and ultimately to the children of the world. For that reason I ask you to share this book with others, to communicate with your family and friends about it, to use the media and the Internet to let others know about it. You may quote it freely, even large sections, whole chapters – I am not interested in being paid for this work, only in its dissemination and spreading it as far and wide as possible. For those who lack the money to purchase a copy, let everyone know that I will continue to offer it free as a pdf to all who email me and ask for it.

And I hope that you may consider how in your life to counteract all the inconsiderate attitudes of our governments and institutions and place our children in center of our hearts and all our actions as a society.

Appendix

The Vision of Elena Balsamo............................. 229
The Circle Way Basics.................................. 235
Pre-History 241
Joyous Childraising 243

The Vision of Elena Balsamo

Elena Balsamo's vision which led her to ask me to make family workshops for her followers – but first, the letter she sent me after we had made workshops with her for three years and I presented her and her editor with the text of this book they had requested:

Dear friends of the Tribe,

I decided to write this letter because, after what was experienced at the Camp, I feel that the time has come for a full opening of the heart.

We are in a very special moment in our history, both socially and individually. I feel I am not alone in having to make that leap that will lead to a total change in my life. For many years now that I'm preparing for this.

I want to give you today words of hope, I want to sew seeds in our fertile land so that they can germinate and bear much fruit.

I'll do it by telling a story: the story behind our project, a very ancient history that has its roots in the past and throws its arms into the future, a story that now is the time to share with you. It's the story of a woman who lived in an Indian village. Her name was "Eagle Feather." She was a medicine woman, daughter of a great chief. It's the story of a woman who lost everything she loved most in the world: her tribe, her family, her land, her companion, the son she carried in her womb.

A chief found her and greeted her in her village, cared for her, and his partner sang a song for her: her voice was so beautiful that she decided to stay and start living again.

This is my story, this is our story, the story of a destroyed village that we now have the task of rebuilding. It is for this reason that we met, my friends.

I was entrusted with the onerous mission to remember (which means "to put in my heart") and transform a story of such great suffering in a love story.

Before the project could be realized I had to overcome, in a sort of initiatory path, a series of steps without skipping any of them. And that's exactly what I did in the last twelve grueling and painful years of my life.

So there was the need to meet Manitonquat (whose name means not for nothing "Medicine Story"!).

All of us together will build the Village of Joy, and will dwell in peace, beauty and harmony with our children, and also Ellika and Manitonquat.

This is the dream that I have treasured in my heart for a long time, which I watered with love and trust and fertilized with patience and tenacity so that we could achieve for the good of everyone.

And today I'm here to tell you that you can. Never give up what you feel deep in your heart, do not lose hope, never let go of the light that burns in you, never trample your dreams because your dreams are the essence of yourself. It's true, it will take work, time, and effort to make them reality, but you can do it and that's what matters. So, courage, my friends!

Thanks for being there and – now I can finally say it – walking with us in Beauty!

Elena

Dear Story,

I want to thank you again for your very precious work with our group: it has been very useful for all of us. Now I know that the project will start and on a day, not so far, we will live all together in our village, the Village of Joy! And we will build a house for you and Ellika so you can come whenever you want and stay with us.

We love you and Ellika so much!

A big hug, Elena

The Hocioka Project, The Village of Joy
The Vision of Elena Balsamo

"We use our minds to understand what type of life we can offer our children."

—Tatanka Yotanka (Sitting Bull)

"Hocioka" (pronounced *ho-choka*) in the language of Lakota American Indians means the empty centre inside the circle of the tepee: a sacred space where the four directions meet.

Hocioka is therefore the centre of the self, the universe, the essence, and the origin of life.

From this empty space, from the point where body, mind, heart, and spirit meet to become One, a vision is born giving life to a whole village. The Village of Joy.

Because joy is the ultimate end to which every human being tends.

Because joy is a spiritual, interior dimension that once attained lasts forever (unlike happiness which is a mental dimension conditioned by external factors).

Hocioka, the Village of Joy is a sort of large living mandala, a symbolic representation of the macrocosm reflecting in itself the one of the inner microcosm: "inside like outside."

The project plan has a circular shape that recalls the Medicine Wheel of Native Americans and like the latter is a journey: it is possible to access it from any point, direction, and bit by bit go through it all to find that Life is completeness and an exchange.

The structure is composed by four main buildings and by a central one representing the heart of the village: "hocioka," the sacred space, an empty space where you can collect your thoughts and that works as an energetic plant for the whole structure.

Four is a sacred number in the majority of the Native American cultures and is a symbol of stability and order.

The four buildings are called "Houses"– in accordance with the Montessori spirit: "The House is first of all a symbolic space reproducing in each of us the sensation of the antenatal space, when our psychophysical system lived protected in an internal soft and circular space, in a dress that fit us perfectly; our first house is in fact the womb. The house is female, is a space inside which is the place that brings life and welcomes it into the world. …Traditionally it is represented by the 'fireplace', and recalls the warmth of affections, becoming also the place that protects physically, and a place of the heart." (Bianca Lepori, Architect)

The Houses are placed in the four sacred directions:

- To the East where life beings, there is the **Maternity House,** which offers help and support to mothers before and after giving birth, during breastfeeding and the first two years of the child's life. Inside the same building there is also a shop called "Babies of the World" where it is possible to find the best products for newborns and babies from all over the world.

- To the South, where you can go down the paths of trust and innocence, the Montessori **House of Children** (for children from 2 to 6 years) and the **Montessori Primary School** are found.

- To the West is found the **Health House**, where introspection and work on the body help you get in touch with Mother Earth and find the body-mind well-being. **The Health House** offers natural medicine consultancy and paths to personal growth through art and movement.

- To the North, where the Ancestors' wisdom is shared for everyone's good, we find the **Culture House**, which offers access to the sources of culture through an intercultural and multilingual Library with a large section for children, a Maternity Museum of

Appendix: The Vision of Elena Balsamo { 233

the different cultures, and an Auditorium for shows and concerts.

On top of these structures there are additional ones, such as:

- The **Reception** (a Welcome Room for visitors) and the administrative **offices**.

- The **Sixth Happiness Inn** (a Hotel equipped with 7 rooms to welcome guests and visitors) and the **Five Continents Trattoria** (a restaurant, with International menus, providing the meals for the children of the school and visitors: every day we serve typical dishes of one continent).

- The **Workshops** where afternoon courses are held for children (singing, martial arts, painting, wood work, cooking, juggling, etc).

- **Sport fields and the swimming pool**
- **The vegetable garden and the educational farm**

Architecture is inspired by Montessori principles. There are four main principles inspiring shapes and spaces: beauty, simplicity, order, and gentleness.

Beauty: *"The spiritual school does not set limits to the beauty of its environment other than economical ones. Beauty inspires concentration and offers rest to the fatigued spirit. The right environment for a human being is an artistic place."* –Maria Montessori

Simplicity, namely the "necessary and sufficient," is nothing more than what is necessary, the essence.

Order and accuracy: order in the environment helps build an internal order, offering calm and security, tranquillity, and peace.

Gentleness can appear rather strange as an architectural principle, but the term here is used with the meaning used by Piero Ferrucci, namely the set of qualities including empathy, contact, care, welcome, warmth, respect, etc., all elements that an architecture generated by the heart – and not just by the mind – is able to evoke as if by magic. An environment permeated with gentleness is a warm, welcoming environment where one feels welcomed, respected and protected, considered and appreciated, listened to and seen; where you feel a sense of well-being simply for the fact of being there.

Here is the reason for the rounded shapes that offer containment, that recall the symbolism of the hug, of female shapes, of the "yin," which for the child represents the extension of the maternal body. Circular shapes that recall the cyclic patterns of life and that recall also the architectural style of the native people of the world (such as the Mongolian Yurt and Hogan Navajos).

Each building has large glass walls – real windows on the world – to open from a safe and welcoming space towards the outdoors, in a sweet and gradual passage from indoors to outdoors.

The buildings are surrounded by large green spaces: meadows and tree areas, small well-kept gardens, such as Zen gardens, with Japanese maples, small hills, little water falls and lakes with wooden bridges and paths connecting to the different areas of the village.

The materials used are natural: stone and especially wood, the material that most of all conveys a sense of warmth and welcome, that makes you feel "at home."

The team of operators of the international and multilingual centre is highly qualified, not just from a professional, but also from a "human" point of view: the team's characteristics are in fact gentleness, empathy, respect, care, and interest, irreducible qualities if you want to make an authentic encounter with others, especially if it is an educational and therapeutic one.

For further information on the project, please contact the author: elena.balsamo@fastwebnet.it

The Circle Way Basics

From the ancient wisdom carried by elders of many indigenous cultures we may distill three basic instructions for a good life, a good society, and a good world. When followed they will maintain human happiness and well-being, benefiting all of life.

The first instruction is respect. Respect reminds us that everything in Creation is one piece, that it is all connected and we are related to it all, that when we touch any part of it we are touching ourselves, when we harm any part we are harming ourselves, and when we heal or help any part we are healing and helping ourselves.

The second instruction is the circle, to add to this respect as much connection and closeness as we are able to make with any part of Creation, and to come together in circles in order to support each other. We want to learn as much as we can about the universe we live in and the other beings that inhabit it with us. We think of this in terms of a circle in which all are connected, all are important, interesting, necessary and sacred. The closeness of our connections, to ourselves, our families, our neighbors and colleagues, to strangers, the plants in the garden, the trees in the forest, the animals, the waters, the winds, the stars, to any and all part of this Creation, fills us with love and joy. This circle extended in time becomes a spiral that enhances the positive evolution of humankind to ever-greater understanding and bliss.

The third instruction is celebration. To be continually aware and give thanks for the wondrous gift of this life and the consciousness by which we are able to perceive it. We can, and often do fail to perceive the wonders about us, but if we make a practice of regular thanksgiving and celebration we remind ourselves that choice is always ours to make every moment.

Also basic to our closeness is our understanding of our nature: how good, how compassionate and kind we all are naturally, how we like to have fun and enjoy each other, when we are not confused by old hurtful patterns getting in our way. How we all want to be helpful, and how the best help we can give others is to listen to them, be a mirror to their true selves and an ally in seeing and discharging negative patterns.

We became human (homo sapiens sapiens) through a process in which our distant pre-human ancestors learned from each other, learned to come together to cooperate for safety and well-being. We seem to have learned that better than other hominid species because they became extinct while our species thrived and lived on in us. Those ancestors developed complex languages that broadened the scope of their brains and their thinking. The full development of our brains takes years, perhaps a quarter of a century, and it takes half of that time for the immature child to be able to survive independent of adults.

This became possible as human beings had learned to stay together, to support each other for survival, in larger than extended family units, in tribal units. For perhaps a hundred thousand years human life developed in these close tribal circles of mutual support.

When a baby was born it was a joy and a gift to the whole tribe, a cause for celebration. Everyone cherished the little children and took pride in their growth and achievements. The whole tribe welcomed and celebrated their coming of age as adults, the unions they made, and the children they bore, and all attended and honored the elders they became.

Of course that model is the one I have learned about from elders who grew up in those traditions in North America. There have also been other tribes in the world where practices that are oppressive and hurtful developed that we would call inhuman, practices growing from hurts and imbalances, from superstition and fear and domination. These tribes appear not to be the norm and certainly were extremely rare in North America.

I am not recommending a return to any of the older traditions, only that we learn from them what was best for human life and see how we may adapt those principles to the world of today.

It seems that closeness to other human beings is essential to our humanity. That closeness needs to be supportive and caring, accepting, and affirming. When children are respected and guided with unconditional love and appreciation this is the way they will interact with others.

The social environments in which we struggle for our survival today are unhealthy, not caring or supportive, not loving or affirming. They are powered by vast economic and political institutions controlled not by love or service to people, but by materialism and greed. They are fixed and entrenched environments that can be influenced only slightly and only by stirring massive movements for change.

People say to change the world we must first change ourselves. Well, yes. But people have been making very positive changes in themselves for several generations now with very little effect on the dominating cultures of the world. It's not that we don't have enough power, it's just not enough to exercise that power in the way we are doing.

Nevertheless there are many who are making big changes at this time. Right now as I write there are thousands all over the world who are building their dreams together. In places like Tamera, Damanhur, Findhorn, The Farm, Christiania, Auroville, and thousands of other communities, newer communities, people are coming together to make lives that may be better for themselves, for their children, for the Earth and the future.

It is not so easy, since we carry with us many of the problems of the cultures we grew up in. The biggest problem we carry, since it affects all the others, is our isolation – from each other and from ourselves.

Again: since it affects all the others, the biggest problem we have is our *isolation* – from each other and from ourselves.

Because of that isolation, because we have not known how to get close enough to each other, we have missed the essential truth of our own power, of our goodness, our love and compassion, our creativity and intelligence, our playfulness and joy in living. By not finding it in others we don't find it in ourselves. We need others not caught up in our distress to be mirrors to us of our true powerful, loveable, and excellent selves! The most effective tool we have developed in that work is what we call Supportive Listening. Through that process we build trust and closeness and are able to discharge our negative hurts and patterns and come to our full power – our authentic selves.

Most importantly we have not fully understood that our failures to make a good society are not our fault. We have not understood that our confusion, our feelings of hopelessness and frustration and depression and all the negative feelings that keep us from knowing and being ourselves, confuse our thinking and our ability to create better environments for ourselves. To create in particular better *social* environments, ones more conducive to our loving, creative, playful natures.

In creating such an environment we must be sure to be inclusive and considerate. If we start treating anyone or anything badly we will only re-create the conditions we are trying to escape. Instead of badmouthing people, let's practice goodmouthing them. Let us notice and appreciate what others are doing. Let's congratulate ourselves for our successes, our creativity, and our positive contributions. Let's praise not only the beauties of nature but also the beauty of our own natures.

For that third instruction it is very, very helpful to remember to appreciate and celebrate each other and ourselves often. We all get stuck in patterns sometimes, get discouraged, confused. We can all use support and encouragement. Let us remind each other – please remind me – how perfectly wonderful and loveable we all are – and celebrate!

In The Circle Way we take time often to celebrate. We make ceremonies of celebration. We celebrate the seasons, we celebrate our lives and the lives of others at important times: birth, the onset of puberty, partnership, receiving an honor, honoring an elder, and departure from the circle of life.

We celebrate people on their birthdays. We ask them to appreciate themselves to us and then we tell them what we appreciate about them. We celebrate teachers and leaders in this way to thank them for their thoughtful service to us and the world. At the end of our camps the clans have celebration circles for each one to appreciate himself and be appreciated by everyone else.

To those who feel to use the designation The Circle Way for their activities: if these instructions of our elders are a part of your activities it would seem entirely appropriate to call what you are doing The Circle Way. When you are together spend some of the time listening to each other and appreciating each other, reporting your successes, sharing your needs, your struggles and your troubles, your plans and hopes for the future, and having fun. In the interest of our extending the connection and closeness of the second instruction I hope that everyone using that Circle Way name would stay close and keep all of the others, and me, informed of how things go.

We make our circles to help each other. That was the purpose of the first circle ever made by our ancestors. We come together in order to help each other.

That is why we are together, and in that we are also helped. The elders always instructed us never to speak disrespectfully of anyone in the circle, never to criticize or denounce another person. Those things are harmful not only to the person at whom they are directed, but to the circle and to the person doing the criticizing or denouncing. They create a disharmony that extends beyond the persons and small circles involved and increase the separation and negativity everywhere they touch.

So members of a circle must agree to this instruction of the elders, otherwise it is not The Circle Way. And if they slip and forget they must be gently and fondly reminded by the others. If we find we disagree with something they are doing, we can discuss our disagreement and why we think it may be incorrect and listen to them and work on coming to an understanding without being critical, blameful, or judgmental of each other.

But what about the criticisms and denunciation of people who are not part of a circle, who do not agree to The Circle Way and to our need to be helpful to each other? Unfortunately we can have no influence over what they do except that of our love and understanding.

Our love teaches us that they are us, that they are completely good and valuable as all human beings are, only they don't know that, and our understanding teaches us that they (like us and all human beings) are afflicted with negative patterns, derived from earlier hurts (for which they are not to blame and which they do not understand) but which may add to their present hurts and confusions and obscure their true loving nature, their desire for harmony and their wish to have fun with us.

I am convinced that if we were able to devote the thought and the time and energy for it, our own caring would eventually slip past those patterns to the person inside who really doesn't want them but needs connection and closeness. If time and opportunity for that are presented, it would certainly be worth a try. If not, it doesn't help to feel bad about it, or to let it discourage us even though it makes us sad. We only must continue on our paths of unconditional loving, connecting, and getting as close as we can wherever we can.

We are the result of nature and nurture, genes and environs. At birth we have all we need to live successful, fulfilled lives. If our environment permits and enhances our growth and learning we will be caring, curious, and creative, and lead productive, satisfying lives, connecting with other human beings who engage in supporting and enhancing each other.

Our power is in the power to choose. We are creatures not just of our genes, but of our environment. We have the power to dream, to plan, and to create an entirely different social environment from the one we live in now. The one we grew up in seems to trap us by isolating us from each other and limiting our dreams.

Let us come together. Let us dream together of how we want our world to be for ourselves and for our children. Let us plan it together. Let us roll up our sleeves and build it together.

And then let us not forget always to celebrate!

TOGETHER THERE IS NOTHING WE CANNOT DO.

Pre-History

My thoughts about how the cooperation that worked well in small circles became domination in civilization.

It was at the time of the beginnings of civilization, before the invention of alphabet and the recording of their histories, that a change in consciousness took place in human societies, begun in those civilizations and spread by violence, force of arms and fear throughout the world in the subsequent ten millennia.

What caused that change in consciousness? Very briefly, as far as I have been able to figure out, these early civilizations occurred by the great rivers in China, the Middle East, and Egypt, where the populations exploded due to the spread of newly developed agriculture in those fertile valleys. Egalitarian, cooperative circles that functioned naturally and easily for millennia became in those regions inundated in a few generations with no form to support them. Tribes, clans, villages of a hundred or so who could know and trust and help one another suddenly were masses in the tens of thousands. Babies who had before been born into a system of mutual support based on love and caring that everyone could rely upon for life now must learn to survive in a world of strangers that one could not trust, a world in which fear was the only common perspective.

In those worlds, without the traditions of families and clans to bind and help one another, it was the physically strongest and most violent who could survive, and societal bonds and attitudes changed from cooperation to domination. That change affected all of life. Instead of being custodians and caretakers of the Earth and all life, the attitude was one of mastery. Only men could be masters and only the physically strongest of them. Women, children, the sick, the elderly, and weaker men all must serve the strong. So it was the warlords who organized the new civilizations, who made the laws and customs of subservience, and paid the armies to enforce them out of the tribute and taxes they collected.

It was a world that honored only power and those who could wield it. The cities and states followed the rule of power in conquering others, building their empires on the backs of slaves, creating a history of continuous warfare and oppression that has continued to this day. The empires rose and fell and rose anew to conquer the peaceful indigenous populations of the world, spreading the attitude that power over is good and inevitable, that people are not good and need to be controlled by fear of punishment, women are not good, children are not good, the weak are not good, independent thinkers and artists are not good, caring kindness, gentleness, compassion are weaknesses (honored perhaps in scripture but denied in action).

But those qualities have been built in to our human nature through the millennia of living in cooperative egalitarian circles where everyone knew each other from birth and babies were the center of the community, the center of life, a center infused with the daring and tenderness, the play and the joy, the curiosity and aliveness of the little children.

Even today the attitudes remain throughout most of the world that babies, while they should be physically protected and cared for, must be dominated mentally, emotionally, and spiritually in order to become fully and adequately human. Adults still have the power and domination belief, that because a child is small and weak it does not know how to be a good human being until it is educated, trained, disciplined, taught, and conditioned to become like her adult masters.

That, of course, is a deeply false idea serving only to perpetuate the mess we have made of this world. It is domination that creates fear and perverts our benign and compassionate natures, and it is equal respect and cooperation that restores them to us.

Joyous Childraising

Excerpt from Return to Creation *by Manitonquat. Copyright 1991 (Written well over 20 years ago, before we created our family camps.)*

It is night again, and we are seated around the fire at our Watuppa Reservation. The sparks dance in the dark air and try to climb above the trees toward the stars. I have just finished telling stories, and the youngest ones are being settled down for the night in their camps.

Tomorrow I will call a children's council. I will tell some more stories then, and the young people will have a chance to discuss their own issues and tell stories. The way to really learn and understand a story is to tell it yourself, and I am hoping that some of these young ones will be able to carry on the lore of our people for the next generation. I was very proud when Tokeem, my eldest son, first stood in this circle and told one of our ancient tales to the other children, feeling this part of the Wampanoag heritage passing from the old ones through me into the future generations. Now my second son, Tashin, has begun learning and telling all the stories too.

Of all the things I want to consider in the talks we are sharing here, it is this one, about our relationship to our children, that is the closest to my heart. I have already said that my two sons are the very center of my life, but it is not only my own children that have such importance to me. Children of all ages enrich, elevate, educate me and fill me with love, hope, and gratitude.

Babies delight me, awe me, and make me feel soft and gentle and nurturing. To hold a baby in my arms connects me more than any prayer to the heart of Creation's mystery. The innocent trust of their sleep brings forth my deepest instincts of protection and caring. The curiosity of big, staring eyes and tiny, groping fists reaching into a vast, unknown world excites me with the potential of all the adventure that exists in the universe. And to have those little fingers grip my finger firmly, to see a big toothless smile light that little face, is to have my heart spring like a dolphin in sudden joy.

Toddlers reawaken my consciousness to the miracles of little ordinary things I never notice. Walking with Raven, the three-year old of our community, you can't just rush down the path to where you are going. You have to go at her pace and look at the wonders around you, the grass, the butterflies, the puddles of water. Sometimes she will squat down and just look at the ground for a long time. If you can forget your goal and your impatience for a little, you go and squat with her and enter her world. There are ants there, busy with a whole different life. And a caterpillar, and a beetle, some interesting holes in the ground, and many little stones. She picks up a stone and looks at it closely. Then, glad for your company in her exploration, she hands it to you. What a marvel is this little stone of green and blue and gray! Set in silver you would praise its beauty and perfection, but here you just stepped on it along with hundreds of other miracles, ground into the earth everywhere you walk. This little child looks at you now for your reactions. She is your teacher, sharing her special world with you, and when you smile back you are the teacher too, sharing the confidence and the love of your years of living on this earth she now wants to explore.

For two years now, Raven has been giving herself instructions in language. Learning the words, saying them over and over, chanting them, crooning them, shouting them. And then the questions. So many questions! So much to learn to be able to care for yourself in a world of so many things, animals, and people. How fast they learn! Every day there are new words, new ideas, new accomplishments. Why, if we all kept learning new words, new ideas, new accomplishments, new skills every day at the rate we learned as infants, we should all be the greatest poets, philosophers, scientists that ever lived!

Joy comes through our contact with human beings and other creatures, with the living earth and sky, and for me, my greatest joys come through my contacts with children. Childraising has been a true joy for me since my first son was born, but I must admit I made a lot of mistakes practicing on other people's children, as a relative, a teacher, or a friend earlier in my life. Fortunately for my own children, they came late in my life after many adventures and learnings with many other children, and particularly after experiencing the child raising philosophy of traditional native people in action.

Children are the heart center of the family, as the family is the heart center of the community and of society. So childraising is a crucial consideration for our survival, crucial to the family, to the community and to society, crucial to the survival of our Indian nations and traditional ways.

I believe with all my heart and mind that the traditional native ways of childraising represent the only ways that human parents have discovered to relate to their children in a healthy and balanced way, consistent with the universal, spiritual principles we have been discussing.

These traditional ways were developed over a million years of tribal living experience. Not only on this continent, but all over the world, natural tribal peoples have lived and transmitted essentially the same beliefs and ways of living from generation to generation with peace and stability, equality and well-being for all members of the community. The experience of living with young people growing to adulthood within these families is, on the whole, one of relaxed enjoyment and delight. That accords with our understanding of the Original Instructions saying that children are our greatest blessing and caring for them is our greatest joy.

For one million years the traditional tribal ways have proved successful in holding together the warp and weft of human society in its natural environment. A mere few thousand years ago the ways of civilization began to rise and have already wreaked such havoc upon the earth that the future of the human species is in serious jeopardy. In the past few decades the quality of life has deteriorated rapidly, and most rapidly in the urban centers that are the very fruit and flower and seed of this civilization.

So it would seem to be in the best interest of all people, no matter what their race or heritage, to learn and adapt to the healthy and balanced old family ways.

What are these traditional ways? Looking at natural tribal groups that survive and resist assimilation in North, Central and South America, Africa, Australia and a few island societies, I would use two words to describe the basic spiritual understanding which underlies all their customs and traditions including the raising of children.

These two words are trust and respect.

In the upper Amazon region of Ecuador, the Aorangi people live as their ancestors lived, a nomadic jungle life of hunting and gathering and gardening, moving their villages when the fragile garden soil gives out. Here we can see traditional childraising uninfluenced by any intrusion of modem culture. The children are happy, lively, involved with interest in all aspects of the community. There are no schools or child care facilities. The children follow older children and adults and learn by watching and trying. Everything in the village is shared, fruit from gathering, meat from hunting, and tools. Children cooperate because this is all they see. The idea of competition is unknown to them. There is no rivalry among siblings. Children have equal rights and are loved and cared for by all adults. They are everybody's children, and they are treated with trust and complete respect.

The concept of trust permeates all, shown by a simple faith in the laws and relationships of Creation. In terms of child rearing this means a trust in the basic goodness, intelligence and resourcefulness of children. In the "civilized" world people do not trust each other, and they do not trust their children. Children grow up in an atmosphere of mistrust. They do not trust others, and they do not trust themselves.

No wonder love is so fragile in that world. No wonder families and communities disintegrate.

Trust is not a quality that can be preached or lectured or inculcated or disciplined into a child. It can be destroyed that way but it can only be fostered by trust, by unconditional love and caring. Babies come trusting into the world, expecting to be kept safe, to be fed, to be warm, to be cuddled and loved. To keep that trust we need only keep faith with that baby's expectations. As soon as we take that baby away from its mother, we are shattering that trust. If that baby does not go on the mother's breast and feel her warmth, hear her familiar heartbeat, and suck of that milk when it is hungry, millions of years of genetic expectations are frustrated.

Let us say that this baby was born at home, or in a very enlightened hospital which gave the mother her baby as soon as it was born. Trust continues. But sometime later the baby goes in a crib. The baby wants to be held and cuddled but suddenly she is alone, looking at the world through bars. In prison already! She doesn't even know what she did wrong!

She cries. Her diaper is changed, and she has been fed.

Why is she crying? She gets picked up and walked about. She stops crying and falls asleep. That was it, she was tired. But why couldn't she sleep? Perhaps she needed the assurance of human contact. She gets put back in the crib. Later she wakes with a start and reaches out for momma. Nothing there. Abandoned again. Heartbroken, she wails. After what seems an eternity someone comes, and the routine repeats. Changed and fed and walked and put back in the crib. Is this living? Hey, warden, when does my parole come up?

Traditional native children are always kept in close physical contact with at first the mother, and then with other family members. The mother holds the baby while she does her work, on her lap or in a sling close to her body. When the baby goes into a cradleboard, she is snuggled warmly with a blanket and propped close where she can watch what her mother is doing. She feels in touch and safe as mother talks and sings to her and lets her know that all is well and as it should be. Trust continues.

At night the baby sleeps at her mother's side. When she wakes for a feeding she will not cry out alone in the dark, she will merely reach out for that dependable breast that is right there. In a tribal situation, if the mother is sick or incapacitated, a wet nurse will be found who can sleep with the baby. Satisfied, the baby sleeps again, her trust undisturbed.

Grandmother is there to hold her, and then an aunt, and a big sister, and the father, grandfather, uncles, brothers, as well as cousins. The baby gets passed around a lot to many friendly, affectionate arms. Trust grows.

When does the baby first experience being alone? When she grows big enough, independent and curious enough, to crawl away on her own. She will try it out just a little way and scurry back. Feeling safe, she will try it a little further and a little further, until the next thing you know she is getting married and having her own baby.

There, in a very short story, is the basic teaching of traditional native childraising. What is that teaching? Stay close, stay available, and let them be.

That is the way of trust.

What about respect? Trust is what the traditional native person feels, and respect is the way the traditional native person expresses that feeling to everything in Creation.

Most people agree that respect is a good thing. What they do not agree on is how to teach it. Respect is not taught by coercion. You cannot demand respect. If you demand it, what you will get will not be respect. It may be fear, or it may be submission, or it may be sullen, covert rebellion. But it is not respect.

Then how do you instill respect in your child? Respect, like trust, like curiosity, comes from within. If you want your child to respect others, you must show respect to your child, to your mate, to your parents, to all your relatives and friends and all their children. Respect is a personal value. Values cannot be taught by lecture, reward, or punishment. They can only be taught by example.

Where values are concerned, I think of myself as a counselor to my children. I cannot force my values on them. I can only offer my thinking as a resource to them. If they are to hire me as an advisor, they must have reason to seek my advice. They must be able to see that my life works well for me and for those around me. I may offer unsolicited opinions, but only once, for information. Repetition is preaching and will not be heard.

When we love our children, when we trust and respect them our children return that love and trust and respect. When we accept and appreciate our children for the miracles of Creation that they are, what they return is acceptance and appreciation. As surely as a wolf cub will imitate its parents, your child will model herself on you and your values.

Creation knows what it is doing. All it requires of adults is that they don't abandon their young. Children don't need a lot of instruction. In fact, they learn best when they are not taught. Creation made them imitators, and that's how they learn most efficiently. Whatever we want them to do or be we have to do or be ourselves.

Of course, eventually they will model many people. But their first models are mother and father. Then brother and sister. Maybe eventually they will want to be like Grandfather or Aunt Ramona or old Henry next door. They probably will try a lot of models before they begin to develop their own way.

Who is their guide in this education? Creation is – which is to say, they are themselves. The impulse comes from within.

Of course, you can put stimulations around them. By your enthusiasm and love you can inspire them. But try to push it too hard and you will meet resistance. You will dampen the desire you want to kindle. Because the impulse to learn must come from within them, not from within you.

That is the way of trust. You trust that all you need to do is love that child, shelter her, feed her, protect her from physical danger, and be available for her when she needs you. Creation takes care of the rest. You don't have to preach or lecture or punish, you don't have to cajole or reward, praise or blame. All you have to do is be there for her, accept her, support her, appreciate her for who she is.

Our people understand that young people, seeking to grow strong and independent, look to sources beyond their parents. That is as it should be. In the old ways of many of our nations, there is often someone other than a parent who is responsible for the guidance of a young person. This might be an aunt or an uncle, a clan mother, clan uncle or grandparent. Beyond the circle out of which the child seeks to grow, this person is teacher, counselor, friend, and ally. This counselor appreciates the young person for what she or he is, as an individual, beyond the reflections of family pride. These teachers prepare the young people for their initiations into adulthood and their responsibilities within the family clan, society, and nation. Their attitude towards their young disciples is one of complete respect and trust.

Perhaps the most terrible aspect of the conquest and domination of our people by the distressed culture with which we all must now contend, is the lack of understanding and appreciation of our traditional native ways. We have so much to be proud of in our heritage, and the wisdom of the old ways of child raising is one of our crowning glories.

This philosophy and way of life are so little known that very few people not raised in that tradition are aware of it. Even native people who are a generation or more removed from that experience no longer understand it. I notice that in today's society childraising does not seem to be a joy to most parents, but a struggle, a bewilderment, and often a frustrating exhaustion. In desperation, parents today abandon their custodial responsibilities to the seduction of an unhealthy contemporary culture, canned entertainment, chemical foods, and a cornucopia of narcotics from caffeine to crack.

Nothing makes me sadder than to visit the home of a contemporary native family and see the kids riveted to the television, sugared and chemical foods on the table, and the parents ordering the young people around and arguing with each other. It's not their fault. They are the victims of the pervasive mental and moral decay of that oppressive, dominant culture.

Of course I don't let on that I don't approve of any of what they are doing. That's not our way. All I can do is talk about these things at our ceremonies in a general way, or at lectures I am invited to make, or write articles that they may someday read. But I can tell what will happen to that family. I know that if that family is joining with others to fight for their rights as natives, they will seek out the traditional ways. They will come to ceremonies and gatherings and listen to their elders. And when they learn of traditional childraising, they will begin to think and to change, and they will begin to come closer together.

I also know that if that family is not interested in recovering its heritage and does not seek it with all its energy, it will begin to disintegrate like the other families of the dominant culture. The generation gap will grow wide and deep. The parents will split up, the kids will leave home. Alcohol and drugs will begin to cripple some of those individuals. Some may escape and fight for their own survival alone, and sadly some may leave far behind the struggles of their own people.

That is why in our war against alcohol and drugs our traditional ways are our best resource. These ways are rooted in the family, not the isolated nuclear family, but the extended family. They are based on relationship, on closeness, on people being committed to each other, being there for each other in times of need. They are based on people helping people, on families helping each other. These traditional ways center first of all upon our children. These ways work well for children, because they provide children with a proud sense of their own worth, with trust and dignity and appreciation. Our children are our best hope for eliminating alcohol and drug abuse forever. This is the crucial struggle for us, because our children are our survival. As the great Hunkpapa medicine man Sitting Bull has said, "Let us put our minds together and see what kind of life we can make for our children."

When I see people ordering their children around like slaves, getting angry and shouting if they don't measure up to the parents' standards, when I see kids being hit or bribed, I feel very sad. Those parents don't trust their children, because they have not been trusted themselves. They don't trust Creation. They don't know what trust is.

I am especially sad when I see modem native parents acting like this, because without realizing it they are imitating the dominant culture's destructive methods that are responsible for the dissolution of the family and the collapse of spiritual values.

That dissolution began when native children were taken from their homes and put in boarding schools. When they went home, they often couldn't even talk with their parents because they hadn't been allowed to speak their native languages at school. Thousands of years of gentle, trusting, traditional childraising were lost to many of our people who began to follow the European models.

The European traditions mistrust all of nature, and they mistrust human nature most of all. The concept of Original Sin is fundamental to European law and custom. According to that view human beings are naturally corrupt, greedy, aggressive, sybaritic and self-indulgent, and their anti-social passions can only be restrained under the threat of punishment or promise of reward.

The fact is, good and bad are social concepts and are meaningless when applied to a newborn infant. A baby is not greedy or corrupt or lazy – neither is it generous or noble.

A baby may be hungry. A baby may be curious. A baby may be tired and confused or energetic and expansive. But a baby has no concept of power, although it may feel frustrated if it is restrained. A baby has no concept of ownership, but will be outraged if you take away something it has a grip on.

Little human beings, besides being fed, kept warm and dry and assured of having safe, familiar care available to them, need to expand and explore. The most important thing about our species comes to the fore early in life. Human beings are endlessly curious. They need to explore themselves and their environment.

It is a real need. When a baby is not allowed to explore, when it is placed in a crib or playpen, when it is told "no-no" to everything it wants to touch, it becomes exasperated and puts out more energy, crying, trying to grab. The adult gets more forceful. Look at it from the baby's view. There's someone ten times bigger than you frustrating your every move. What kind of a world is this, anyway?

A better move is to baby-proof the environment and let the child have some scope. This means putting everything dangerous or really valuable out of the way. But don't go too far and remove all possible interests and stimulations, or you will turn the whole house into a barren jail, in which case baby loses interest. The searching brain is confronted with nothing to learn, and she is craving to learn, every minute of her waking life. With no stimulation the child becomes bored and slows down. Later on people will call her stupid. She started out as intelligent as anyone, with a whole universe of potentiality before her. Her body was fed, but not her mind, and so it atrophied, withered from lack of use.

When a person's natural curiosity is allowed full play, learning takes place at an amazing rate. Look at how quickly everyone learns to speak. The more talking the child hears in her home, the faster she learns. But if someone tried to teach a baby to talk with lectures and exercises and homework, if the methods we use to teach writing or arithmetic or history in school were used to teach talking, it would take the child years to learn to speak, and then probably with difficulty.

When someone tells you, "Learn this!" you will have no curiosity about it at all. You will work to learn it if you have to, but your heart won't be in it. Your curiosity comes from inside you as a response to something interesting in your environment – as long as it's not forced on you. When your curiosity is aroused, it gives you a lot of energy. You won't stop until you have learned all you can to satisfy that curiosity, and in the process you'll get curious about something else.

That's how Creation works. Nourished by love and acceptance, encouraged by the availability of grown-up allies, and strengthened by curiosity, children grow into powerful and creative adults who will give the same nurture and appreciation to their children. That is the way of trust.

But what of conflicts? Whenever people live together, as in a family, conflicts arise from time to time. Does the traditional native parent just let the child have her own way all the time, even at the expense of the rest of the family?

Here again the guides are respect and trust. The person in the parenting or teaching role allows the child full independence and autonomy. The child will be allowed to find her own way and make her own mistakes. The child will always know, however, that some responsible adult is available for advice and assistance whenever the child may seek it. Help is neither offered nor withheld, but it is always available.

If what the child wants unavoidably conflicts with the needs or wishes of the parent? They will seek a solution together in an atmosphere of mutual respect. This feeling of respect is so high in a traditional native home that no child would conflict with what that child knew to be of great importance to an elder. And no elder would stand in the way of what the elder knew to be of great importance to a child, for what is important to the child provides the learning and growth that will one day sustain the people and the nation. In such an atmosphere, conflict is very rare and solutions are not difficult to find.

Now, those statements sound too ideal by a lot, I know, and I need to say a few more things to give a little life and reality to that picture. The picture is, in the whole, a true one, as I have observed it in homes of traditional native families throughout North America. I should also say that this is true to the degree that that family is remote from the pressures of the dominant culture of the country, be it Anglo or Latino. In the context of traditional spiritual trust and respect, there is a gentleness, a warm, humorous, and relaxed quality that is a world apart from the tensions and conflicts of the average "civilized" home, be it rich or poor, middle class or working class, suburban or rural. The dominant culture gives only lip-service to children.

Parents are isolated and given no assistance, but are told they are responsible for the care and for the behavior of their children. Parents are afraid to take their children anywhere – they are not wanted in most places. They have no place where the parents work; where children are tolerated, there are severe restrictions on them. Going to some place to work is described as having a career, but taking care of a home and children is not. In a culture that places its values on the amount of recompense, childcare and teaching are underpaid and undervalued, and parenting is unpaid and unvalued. Parents are the last oppressed group to recognize their own oppression and to struggle for their liberation, largely because they are so isolated.

The young people of today are also an oppressed group.

The oppression is enforced in families and schools by denial of any respectful attention, invalidation of their thinking and feelings, misinformation, physical abuse, negative attitudes and low expectations, and economic dependency. Young people have few rights beyond that of freedom from physical battering. Their space and their persons are not respected. They are not paid just compensation for their labor. They are not listened to. Their feelings are not considered important. They are not prized, appreciated, and encouraged in what they do. As babies, though they are constrained, they are thought cute and lovable. But the older they get, the less they are cherished, honored, and treasured for the wonderful human beings they are.

This oppression of young people keeps all of society from the advantages of youthful clear thinking and high hopes for the world. Young people are naturally loving, intelligent, creative and full of fun when they are free of the dismal conditioning of society's institutions. Since young people are half of the world's population, with the encouragement and support of the rest of us, in a short time they could change the world into a more joyous and human place for us all.

In the supportive environment of a community based upon the sacred circle, a community in which the rearing, the care and education of children is shared by aunts and uncles, grandparents, older siblings and cousins, clan members and the community as a whole, there is not a lot of time and attention required from a parent or from anyone person. But until we have been able to recreate our communities as sacred circles, it would help if each one of us would give some extra thought and a little more of our time and attention to the children around us. They are indeed all our children after all. And there is much that one person can do which can be of memorable importance in the life of a child.

How can we be better allies for parents and for young people today? I think this is the important question. We can be better allies for parents if we can take some time to give them attention. Parents and non-parents need to understand the oppressive conditions of parenting and join together to support each other and share childcare. We can play with young people more, take more interest in their interests, follow their leadership and initiative.

We can honor their feelings and encourage their expression. There are so many ways adults deny the expressions of children's feelings. When they are angry, we tell them to be "nice." When they are sad, we tell them to cheer up, everything is all right. When they are afraid, we tell them there's nothing to be afraid of. Adults don't like feeling those feelings, so they deny them in their children. They don't realize that the expression of the feeling is not the hurt but the healing of the hurt.

Probably your own childhood was not exactly as you would have wished. Probably you were not always respected and cherished by the adults around you. This is true to some extent for all of us. But now we have a chance to make a big difference in the lives of children and in the future of the world.

We can offer to all young people of any age complete respect as a full human being. We can value them as unique, independent creatures with ideas and desires of their own. It is important for young people to have one person who respects them, who has no prior expectations about what the shape and form of their lives should be, who applauds them for trying out new things, who doesn't get upset when they are distressed, who knows that their distress is not who they are.

Children come into the world joyously, expecting it to be fun, expecting us to be fun, and to play with them. But we have grown old and serious. Children can teach us to be joyous again. Children are excited to be alive, and they need to see people who are as excited about their being alive as they are.

Let us try our magic feather again. Take hold of it with me now, and we will be transported to a traditional community that lies far from here. It is familiar to me, yet it is not any single community but a composite of many, and the family we visit is a composite of many traditional families I have known, from Akwesasne in New York to Third Mesa in Arizona, from Alaska to Guatemala.

There is a ceremony in the village today, and many relatives have gathered for the occasion. As a result there is a larger herd of children than usual running together in the road and across the field. They run to us as we approach and surround us. Their eyes are merry as they boldly ask us who and what we are, and they giggle at our answers. This is not mockery or malicious laughter, but simple joy at a surprising and endlessly funny world.

Now they have cleverly wormed it out of me that I am a storyteller, and they won't let us escape without a story. After one story, I notice that the crowd of children sitting around listening intently has more than doubled as mysteriously the news of storytelling has spread like a net and drawn in every last child in the village. These are children who are used to storytelling and listen with rapt concentration.

As we finish, we walk into the village surrounded by a great horde of shouting, laughing children. Some call out the news of who and what we are to any within earshot. Others delegate themselves to run home and tell their families. Soon invitations are coming from all sides, borne back by little emissaries from their parents. We accept the first invitation and follow a pack of a half-dozen assorted siblings to their small, family house.

The father greets us outside with a big glad-to-see-you grin and ushers us in. Another gracious smile from the mother inside welcomes us. She gestures at the table, the father speaks a couple of words in the native language, and the children bring up chairs for us to sit, bring bowls of stew from the mother at the stove, and stand around to encourage us to eat. The stew is as comforting and nourishing as the atmosphere of this generous and friendly home.

Soon relatives begin to come in and out the door. All greet us. Some sit with us at the table and are immediately given a bowl of stew. The invariable custom in any native home is: greet the guests and feed them right away.

People begin to coalesce into groups: women with women, men with men, children running in and out. Faces appear and disappear at the doors and windows. Yet the atmosphere is not one of noise and confusion, but relaxed and easy-going. Conversations are quiet and slow, punctuated with little bursts of laughter. Work is being done, jobs being taken without assignment or organization.

Soon we all are on our way to the ceremonies. Several children explain to us what will happen, what we will see, what the songs and the dances and the games will be and what they mean. The children all dance. As soon as they can toddle they begin to imitate the others, hopping and stomping. Then the elders speak. Long speeches in the native language. Everyone listens quietly, including the older children who have begun to understand the importance of these ways and the greatness of this heritage. The little children run around the outside of the circle or climb on family laps. Between the speeches there is a lingering silence as the words of the speaker sink quietly into the minds of the listeners, into their feeling places, into the grass and stones, into the soil of the earth, and then spread away like the thinning smoke of the fire onto the winds of the universe.

Following there is a feast. Everyone has had some hand in it, preparing food or building fires or cutting wood, and this is the culmination of all that community activity. The children are brought to a separate table and served – reminding us that we are here to serve Creation's future. The old people sit and are served. Everyone else gets in line. There is a lot of good food and lots of joking. It is another good day, as it has been for thousands of years among our people.

Our new friends have invited us to stay on and spend the night, and we accept. At home the children of the family ask for a story again, but we say we'd like to hear some of their stories now. The oldest child tells a favorite story, looking to grandfather now and then, who corroborates with a nod and a grunt. Then grandfather tells a story and asks me if we have a story like that. Then I tell one of our stories on a similar theme, and so the evening goes until one by one people grow tired and withdraw for the night. Sleeping children are carried away to bed, and we are left alone.

It has been a slow and easy day despite the excitements of visitors and ceremonies. Nothing pressed or rushed, everything proceeding at a comfortable pace with plenty of time for joking and playing. There's no hurry. Stepping out of the goals and schedules of civilization, we are back in a world without time. The earth, the sun and the stars are not in a race. The life of the people is ageless, and every moment is a perfect eternity.

And what of the children of this family? They seem to live more in the adult world than the children of the dominant culture. They have no special playroom or playground (and in the oldest, most isolated communities they would have no schoolhouse). The world is not separated into adult's and child's. The child learns and finds her way in a unified world, her people's world. There are not great varieties of toys. The implements of play are found in the world, except for a few toys made by the child or by a relative: a doll, a small bow and arrows. Mostly the toys are real tools, growing in size as the child grows. These few objects of play and learning are more prized and appreciated by traditional native children, more cared for and more used than other children's closetsful of manufactured toys that have been purchased from vast retail emporiums upon the overloaded hawking of advertisements and now lie broken or abandoned in favor of some newer interest.

Most of all, these children are not treated in a special way reserved only for children, except in concerns for their feeding and safety. They are full people treated with the respect due to persons of all ages. All day we have not heard the special language and tone we hear addressed to children in the dominant culture: no baby talk, no ordering around, no shouting, coaxing, wheedling, no bribery, sarcasm or demeaning put-downs. Correction of mistakes or dangerous behavior comes gently, casually, with no blame or tension, from whomever is near, older brother or sister, grandmother, uncle, friend. No conflicting relationships have been established. Father has no expectations, makes no demands, so there is no need for separation, rebellion. Father and mother trust their children will learn and figure out the world for themselves, and become the best of what they can be if they are allowed to find their own way.

That is respect. And trust.

These children are not as loud and explosive as children of the dominant culture because they do not have to fight an oppressive system. They do not have to let off steam after being suppressed at desks and forced to pay attention to uninteresting things for precious hours of their young lives while outside the windows important things are happening: chickadees are playing, the arbutus is peeping up through the snow, and all over the civilized world teachers are describing the conquests of Julius Caesar to kids who are learning only that the world is a crazy place, and the things adults value are really dumb.

There are no professional teachers in this traditional village and no professional babysitters. Everyone is available to the children as a resource of knowledge, as an ally and helper, as a protector. No one has to get paid to keep the children out of everyone's way in their own special world. The kids are living and growing in the world with everyone else.

If the children get too loud or wild, the request for consideration comes with the same respect that one would use for the same request of an adult. Adults understand that children tend to be more energetic and more experimental than adults and are in general more tolerant and indulgent than adults of the dominant culture. It is not that they love their children more, but only that their love is expressed through a long tradition of respect and trust. They know babies love to bang pots and scatter them all over the floor and that, while noisy and messy, the benefit to the child is far greater than the small inconvenience to the adult, so they allow them this great pleasure.

They don't worry over their health and safety obsessively, by insisting that they eat and drink in certain ways, or forbidding access to places of imagined danger. Adults in this traditional village trust that as soon as children can feed themselves they will eat as much as they need. They trust that as soon as children can dress themselves they will quickly learn how much to wear to keep warm and dry.

They trust, and thousands of years of living has borne out this trust, that children are naturally intelligent enough and resourceful enough that, once apprised of the danger, they will not burn themselves on stoves, stab themselves with knives, or do any of the things dominant culture parents imagine and worry about constantly.

Traditional native kids don't do any of those things. They are smarter and more responsible than that. Because people aren't always telling them what to do and what not to do, they figure things out a lot earlier and become more self-reliant at a younger age than most children in society today.

Because becoming responsible is a mark of growing up, they follow the ways of other children a year or so older. In this way, when the time comes, children learn jobs that fit into the life and work of the family and of the community.

That's why today we didn't see a lot of organizing. Suggestions are made to children in a friendly way. If the child does not respond, she probably isn't old enough. If he is old enough, perhaps a parent may talk to him, still in a respectful trusting way. If there is the slightest feeling by the child of oppression, then it will be better if grandfather, or an uncle, or older brother or a friend should talk to him. Someone that he trusts has no oppressive intention, no program or expectations, and speaks only from friendship can sometimes make suggestions more easily. These ways can still be found in the remote areas, away from civilization. In many places civilization is moving close, claiming the children for its schools, luring the families (impoverished by the theft of their land and resources) into the cities and the ranks of unemployment and welfare. In those places it's hard to live the old ways. It's not that these traditional values cannot be maintained in a family that has a lot of contact with the dominant culture, but such a family must be more conscious of the threats to its values and more zealous in protecting them.

One such family I have known is that of Janet and the late Don McCloud in the Puyallup and Nisqually area of Washington State. This family has been engaged in the struggle for their people's rights, including fishing rights, since the early sixties, aided by such allies as Dick Gregory and Marlon Brando, as well as native leaders and warriors from many nations. Being the focus of so much tension and attention has naturally been a burden at times. Because of their continued espousal of traditional spiritual values, and the help of native spiritual leaders from all over Turtle Island, and due to the acute intelligence and fiery stamina of Janet, and the gentle, good-humored strength of Don, they became an example to all of endurance under tremendous pressure. It is a great fortune and strength for my family here in the East to have known and been inspired by these good friends of the West for so many years, and it was a great privilege for me to have performed a traditional wedding ceremony for two of their daughters.

Barbara, Janet's youngest daughter, has now grown to leadership in her people's interests and edits a journal for northwest native women. When she was quite a young girl she illustrated in an unexpected way to me the respect taught in that family. At the United Nations Habitat conference in Vancouver, British Columbia, we had an native spiritual gathering convened by a number of traditional Hopi elders who had caravanned from Arizona. Our friend Thomas Banyacya had a statement from the elders which he hoped to deliver at a meeting in the Queen Elizabeth Theatre. The natives all went to listen, but we were not allowed entrance to the hall. The management seemed to be afraid of so many natives, even though we said we were a peaceful spiritual gathering. They decided to let a few people in, one at a time, and many non-natives, used to protests and occupations, crowded to the entrance. The natives mostly stayed back and watched.

The exception was my young friend Barbara McCloud.

Being small, she slipped and squirmed unnoticed through the crowd jam until she was in front of the door. When it was her turn to go in she stood fast, refusing to enter and not letting anyone else go in past her.

I didn't notice this at first. All I could tell from where I was behind the crowd was that there was some commotion. Then someone passed the message that the door guards wanted me to go up there, and the crowd opened a grudging path for me. I thought they wanted me to arbitrate some dispute, and I was surprised to find that it was little Barbara blocking the door.

"Would you please go in, sir?" the guard pleaded, "This little girl says she won't go in until her elder goes in."

I looked at Barbara. She glowed with quiet inner strength as she regarded the guard with a resolute stubbornness, but there was a hint of a conspiratorial smile as she glanced at me. We shared a deep, ancient secret and a power.

I took her arm, and we went in together.

Changing the World

It's about an extreme makeover for this world.
I got this friend – Mike? Always a big smile
Because he is changing the world.
Relaxed. Thoughtful. Having fun.
So what is it works for you? I say.
Five steps, he says. And here they are.

First step is discharge. Discharge, discharge.
If you bottle up your feelings you lose.
Lose your energy, confuse your mind,
Pretending, you're just on automatic.
Tap that terror, that rage, those tears,
Turn loose in a safe place, with someone
Who listens, understands, encourages you.

Second step: Fall in love with everyone –
Fall in love with everyone you meet.
Sounds good, but sounds hard. It's not.
People are really lovable after you pass
The things that terrorized and frustrated them.
I know what you mean, Mike, I been
Doing it years now and it works for me.

Third step: Study the problem. That's work.
The problems are huge. But I'm a student –
All my life I watch, I listen, I read,
I learn, little by little, and it helps
To figure out why things got to this mess,
And how we might start to untangle it.

Fourth step: Have a vision. How you want
The world to look, how it should be
If it ever were to be fit for human life
And happiness, how we want it
For ourselves - especially for the children.
Make it impeccable, your dream, why not?
It could happen, since we all want it.

Last step: Get to work. Get off your duff,
Roll up your sleeves, start to build the dream.
Not alone – we need each other, we need
People in our world. But we all want peace,
Health, happiness, love, enough for all,
No one left out of the dream – OUR world.

So thanks, Mike. I am doing it.
I let out my feelings with close friends,.
I fall I love every day with more and more.
I keep watching, listening, reading, learning,.
I have woven a dream of us all together,
And I have been working at that for years.

But relaxed says Mike – that's good.
It doesn't help to get too tense, I know.
So I smile at the promise of something to do,
And I laugh and play with all the children.
I remember to keep getting closer to everyone,
Love the Earth, life, myself, and have more fun.

Dedicated to Mike Markovitz, Re-evaluation Foundation

Bibliography

Re-Evaluation Counseling

Most of the tools we work with were developed by Re-evaluation Counseling. Their materials can be purchased from Rational Island Publishers, 719 Second Avenue North, Seattle, WA 98109. www.rationalisland.com

Pamphlets

How Parents Can Counsel Their Children, Tim Jackins
Listening Effectively To Children, Patty Wipfler
The Art of Listening, Harvey Jackins
Family Work, P. Wipfler, D. Shisk, T. Jackins, L. Kenny, Cesar, L. Garcia, & E. Brown
Permit Their Flourishing, The Staff of The Palo Alto School
Understanding And Supporting Young People, Jenny Sazama

Journals

The Caring Parent – Issues 1 through 6 available
Young And Powerful – Issues 1 through 7 available

Audio CDs

Being Effective Allies to the Very Young, Tim Jackins
A Description of RC Work with Young People, Tim Jackins

DVDs

How Parents Can Counsel Their Children, Tim Jackins
Counseling the Very Young, Tim Jackins
An Introduction to Re-Evaluation Counseling & Family Work, Tim Jackins

Other Books

Children in Our Culture

Their Name Is Today: Reclaiming Childhood in a Hostile World, Johann Christian Arnold
(A book I discovered that came out after I wrote this one which contains good important thinking about how today's culture acts against children. Read it!)

Supportive Science & Research

Why Love Matters, Sue Gerhardt
Mothers And Others, Sarah Blaffer Hrdy
How Humans Evolved, Robert Boyd & Joan B. Silk
The Evolution of Childhood, Melvin Konner
Scientific Secrets For Raising Kids Who Thrive, Peter M. Vishton, (*The Great Courses*, on CDs or DVDs)

Playing With Children

Playful Parenting, Lawrence J. Cohen
The Art of Roughhousing, Anthony T. Benedet & Lawrence J. Cohen
Playful Learning, Mariah Bruehl
How To Play With Your Children, Brian & Shirley Sutton-Smith
The New Games Book, New Games Foundation
Living Joyfully With Children, Win & Bill Sweet

Discipline

Discipline Without Distress, Judy Arnall
Positive Discipline, Jane Nelson
Loving Your Child Is Not Enough, Nancy Samalis with Martha M. Jablow
Unconditional Parenting, Alfie Kohn

Other Favorites of Mine

Peaceful Parents, Happy Kids, Dr. Laura Markham
Connection Parenting, Pam Leo
Raising Our Children, Raising Ourselves, Naomi Aldort
The Philosophical Baby, Alison Gopnik
Parent Effectiveness Training, Thomas Gordon
Simplicity Parenting, Kim John Payne, M.Ed with Lisa M. Ross
The Natural Child, Jan Hunt
Attachment Parenting, Katie Allison Granju with Betsy Kennedy

For Optimum Growth of Children

Children: The Challenge, Rudolf Deicers, MD
Helping Young Children Grow, Susan E. Warrell
The Optimistic Child, Martin E. Seligman
Help! For Parents of School-Age Children and Teenagers, Jean Lilly Clarke
Giving The Love That Heals, Hartville Hendrix & Helen Hunt,

Older Classics

Magical Child, Joseph Chilton Pearce
Magical Parent/Magical Child, Michael Melissa & Joseph Chilton Pearce
The Drama of The Gifted Child, Alice Miller
Banished Knowledge, Alice Miller
How Children Learn, John Holt
Growing With Your Children, Herbert Kohl
How To Parent, Fitzhugh Dodson
Natural Parenthood, Eda J. Leshan
Tomorrow's Children, Riana Eisner
The Continuum Concept, Jean Liedoff
Liberated Parents/Liberated Children, Abel Faber & Elaine Mulish

The Fun Book of Fatherhood, Jerry Commarata
   with Frances Spatz Leighton
Play Therapy, Virginia Maxline

The Village

Changing the World, Manitonquat
Have You Lost Your Tribe?, Manitonquat
Calling the Circle, Christina Baldwin
Creating a Life Together, Diana Leafe Christian
Ecovillage Living, Hildur Jackson
Ecovillages, Jan Bang
Ecovillages, Jonathan Dawson
Wisdom Circles, Charles Garfield, Cindy Spring, & Sedona Cahill
The Spirit of Intimacy, Sobonfu E Somé
The World I Dream Of, ed. Curt Butz
   (various authors including Manitonquat)

Resources

Patty Wipfler: www.handinhandparenting.org
Lawrence J. Cohen PhD: www.playfulparenting.com
Pam Leo: www.connectionparenting.com
Dr. Laura Markham: www.ahaparenting.com
Althea Solter: www.awareparenting.com
Jennifer Kolari: www.connectedparenting.com
April Perry & Saran Loosli: www.powerofmoms.com
Mark Brady: www.committedparent.wordpress.com
Lori Petro: www.teach-through-love.com
Alice Miller: www.alice-miller.com
Manitonquat (Medicine Story): www.circleway.org
Re-Evaluation Counseling: www.rc.org
European Resource: www.connected-childhood.de

About the Author

Manitonquat (Medicine Story) is a storyteller, an elder and a keeper of the lore of the Assonet Band of the Wampanoag Nation of Massachusetts. Author of ten published books and a former columnist and poetry editor with the internationally acclaimed journal *Akwesasne Notes*, he has also edited *Heritage*, a journal of Native American liberation. He continues to develop tools for creating a more humane society based upon teachings of the elders of the First Nations and the explorations of his camps under the designation The Circle Way. They have a website at www.circleway.org.

Manitonquat has spoken to peace conferences and groups on three continents, was the keynote speaker at the United Nations observance of the 50th anniversary of Gandhi's assassination, directs prison programs for native spirituality, advises a nature school, and, with his wife Ellika, makes workshops and annual international family camps and advises new communities in ten European countries and the US.

"The work that you have been engaged with over the many years – raising Communities in centered humanity – spirituality – is really at the Heart of the Sacred and the greater promise for the future. …maintaining a People's History is both a fine art and an evocative response to the incoherence, tyranny, and cynicism of modernity.

"Manitonquat is one of the Wampanoag Nation's leading national treasures."

– Comments about Manitonquat from gkesedtanamoogk, Wampanoag elder and teacher of Native Studies at the University of Maine

Printed in Great Britain
by Amazon